LLC & S-CORPORATION & TAXES BEGINNER'S GUIDE

5-in-1 Book

Everything on How to Start, Manage Your Company and Reduce Your Taxes. Includes Accounting 101 & Bookkeeping Guide

Steven Carlson

TABLE OF CONTENTS

INTRODUCTION

Welcome to the beating heart of your entrepreneurial aspirations: the definitive guide to LLCs and S-Corporations tailored for the savvy small business owner. You're about to embark on a journey that could redefine your business and propel it into the stratosphere of success. Whether you're a veteran business connoisseur or a neophyte with a dream clasped tightly in your hands, let this comprehensive manual be the beacon that guides you through the fog of corporate complexity.

In these pages, you will discover the nuances of Limited Liability Companies (LLCs) and S-Corporations—structures designed not only to shield but to empower. We'll start with the nuts and bolts, forging a robust understanding of what it truly means to form an LLC or S-Corp. From there, we'll navigate the labyrinthine corridors of management, taxes, accounting and bookkeeping all the while dispelling the myths and spotlighting the strategies that ensure smooth sailing for your business.

But this guide isn't just a cold list of statutes and regulations. We cater to the flesh and blood behind-the-scenes, speaking directly to you—the fearless entrepreneur ready to stake a claim in the world of commerce. Through a narrative that's as engaging as it is informative, we keep the conversation flowing, ensuring that every slice of wisdom is served with a side of personable guidance. With every turn of the page, your confidence will swell as you glean insights on how to shield your business assets, all while ensuring your financial ship doesn't spring a leak due to tax liabilities or haphazard accounting mistakes. This guide illuminates the path to leveraging legal structures to your benefit, ensuring the fruits of your toil are safeguarded beneath the steadfast canopy of your chosen corporate form.

The knowledge contained here will demystify the often-intimidating world of deductions, credits, and incentives, arming you with practical acumen to orchestrate a tax strategy harmonized with the goals of your enterprise.

So, take this moment at the prelude of our collaboration to savor the anticipation, for you stand on the precipice of transformative understanding. We invite you to turn these pages with the voracity of a pioneer venturing into unexplored territories, eager to claim the wisdom that awaits. Let's raise the curtain together on this enlightening exploration.

LLCs and S-Corps are more than mere business entities; they're vessels for your dreams and ambition. Here is your ticket to a future where you steer the ship, navigating through the waters of corporate law and taxation, destined for the horizon of your business' fullest potential.

Ready? Set your sights on the chapters ahead, and let's delve into the essence of what it means to be a tactically informed and forward-thinking small business owner. Welcome aboard this voyage of discovery, where knowledge indeed becomes your gateway to financial freedom.

We invite you to scan this "QR code"

<u>By using the camera of your phone aiming at the QR code and clicking on the link that appears</u>

SCAN TO CLAIM YOUR BONUSES

OR

ENTER THIS URL IN YOUR WEB BROWSER:

bit.ly/psgy

(only use lowercase letters)

SECTION I
LLC & S-CORPORATIONS

CHAPTER 1
LLC EXPLAINED

What Exactly Are LLCs and How Do They Work?

Let's look at the first "L," limited, then the second L liability, by way of an example.

If you have a small car accident, a fender bender let's say, and you are at fault, then you are liable for the damage to the other driver's car. If you are insured, you are still liable, but that liability is limited. Your insurance company will pay for the damage; however, you will need to cover the collateral, also referred to as "the excess." That collateral (excess) will most likely be less than the cost to repair the other driver's vehicle, but, if you are not insured at all, you are liable for the entire repair bill.

This is just an example to illustrate the terms, "limited," and "liability," so it has nothing to do with companies, but it creates an understanding of the concept.

Ask yourself a simple question, "Do I want to be less liable, or more liable?" I am sure you will choose the former, so let's apply the concepts specifically to companies. Consider the fact that there are many people out there, who will register an LLC, but tacitly waive the personal legal protection by signing personal surety. Never do that—I will come back to this topic.

The term LLC refers specifically to companies in the U.S., so if you are in other parts of the world, the terms may be, "Proprietary Limited," or "Limited Liability Partnerships," but the structures are very similar.

So, what exactly is an LLC? An LLC, short for Limited Liability Company, stands as a legal entity chosen by U.S. business owners to govern their operations. The establishment of an LLC serves as a safeguard for individual or group members' personal assets, shielding them in the event of legal challenges or bankruptcy.

Additionally, it offers flexibility in terms of taxation, recognizing that businesses vary in their operational structures. Some may opt for taxation resembling a sole proprietorship, while others may choose to be taxed as a corporation.

A sole proprietorship is a straightforward, unincorporated business model owned and operated by a single individual. It stands out as the simplest and hassle-free structure available, allowing the sole owner to claim all the business profits. In this uncomplicated setup, there are no complexities or formalities—just a direct and straightforward ownership arrangement.

A sole proprietorship is owned by a single individual with personal liability, while an LLC provides limited liability protection and allows for multiple owners.

Difference Between LLCs and Corporations

Selecting the appropriate business structure, particularly between an LLC and a corporation, is a crucial decision when establishing your business (we'll be exploring this in greater detail in chapter 2). This choice ensures that you adopt a structure aligning with the size and requirements of your business. Whether you opt for an LLC or a corporation, both provide numerous benefits, including liability protection, a well-defined operating framework, and enhanced credibility for your newly formed company.

For both of these business structures, you'll need to complete business formation paperwork with the state, ensuring personal liability protection for company owners. Generally, corporations adopt a more standardized and inflexible operational structure, accompanied by increased reporting and recordkeeping demands compared to the more flexible LLCs. LLC owners enjoy a greater degree of freedom in shaping their business operations.

On the tax front, LLCs offer more versatility than corporations. LLCs aren't confined to a specific tax classification, providing options to be taxed as sole proprietorships, partnerships, C corporations, or S corporations.

When it comes to ownership, transferring shares in a corporation is notably simpler than transferring ownership interests in an LLC. This factor renders corporations an attractive choice for business owners seeking external investors.

Major corporations are like LLCs on steroids, and offer the same protection; however, they are intrinsically complicated, and the domain of the, "Good 'Ol Boys." I suppose you could say that LLCs are a lay person type of entity, to be broadly colloquial.

As I said earlier, an LLC can be seen as a person, and it is very possible that an LLC can be in serious debt, but you, as a separate person but also as a member of the LLC, are not liable for one cent of the company debt. There are some exceptions, but I'll get to those in good time.

To break it down in a practical sense, let's say that a businessman by the name of Jim White, is the sole member of an LLC called JW Trading. The LLC has been in existence for 10 years, and Jim has made a comfortable living from the company. He has managed to pay off his mortgage and buy himself several vintage cars. He basically has no debt in his personal capacity.

JW Trading loses a major contract, and quickly gets into significant debt, but Jim was smart enough to make sure that JW Trading never acquired any assets whatsoever. This means that creditors can sue the pants off JW Trading, and get legal judgments against the company, but cannot repossess the company's assets because there aren't any.

Jim's liability is 100% limited, so his house and cars are safe, in addition to any other assets in his personal name. I am often asked if a wife or husband of the LLC member can be personally liable. The answer is obvious because that person has no involvement, so liability is not even up for discussion.

Back to Jim, the only issue he may face is that he no longer has an income; however, he could start another business, or sell some of his cars, to maintain a good lifestyle.

This might sound a bit unfair but remember that the legislation intends to provide personal protection, and Jim has operated within the law, so he has not done anything to compromise his morals. All he has done is operated in a smart manner, by using the benefits of an LLC.

Fundamentally, LLCs, by their very nature, offer asset protection, and in the above hypothetical case, Jim has protected his personal assets. If you want to be exact in a simple sense, you could refer to an LLC, as a "personal asset protector."

Pros and Cons of Starting an LLC, in General

Most of us make pro and con lists, and if we don't, then we should. It is a very simple, yet effective way to assist in decision making. This is even more applicable when starting a business, and trying to work out what structure will operate most effectively, in your specific situation.

Arguably the biggest pro is taxation, which differs slightly depending on the number of members of the LLC. A single member LLC, such as JW Trading, is taxed as a sole proprietorship, whereas a multiple member LLC is taxed as a partnership. These terms are basically semantics, and in very simple terms, whether there is one member, or seven members, each member is taxed in their personal capacity, but only on profits.

Consider this, general employees will often receive medical care benefits that are covered by the companies that they work for, and exactly the same applies to members of LLCs. So, the company pays, thus, personal profit is reduced and so is tax liability.

Another pro is that there are less rules, so to speak. Decision making processes are widely discretionary and members can essentially do what they like, in terms of company management and possibilities.

There are no shareholder resolutions, or meeting attendance quotas, or the need to get a whole bunch of signatures before doing anything. The private sector bureaucracy is eliminated, and nobody enjoys bureaucracy; except the bureaucrats, who do their best to do as little as possible, at the slowest pace possible.

Also, LLC as a suffix to your company's name, adds credibility. JW Trading, LLC sounds more professional and official than just JW Trading. I would compare it to registering your own domain, as opposed to having a Yahoo.com email address. A small pro, but a pro nonetheless.

There is also some wiggle room in terms of profit sharing, and whilst share certificates are often drafted in LLC's, they are not a requirement, so profit share agreements in multiple member LLCs can differ from month to month. It can be said to follow the old KISS analogy, Keep It Simple Stupid.

You may have started to wonder when the cons were coming…Well here they are. Cost is a potential con, and certainly depends on which state your LLC is registered in. As you can imagine, in California, the registration fees are outrageous, and on top of those, the annual renewal fees are just as bad. But taxation is also very stringent and limiting; your taxes will be high. This con is semi-mitigated, and profit declaration through large company expenditure is the silver lining.

I suppose you could say that such cons are more prevalent in some states than others, and the same applies to resignation of old members, and appointment of new members. In Michigan for instance, if a member resigns, the company has to be dissolved and re-formed, which is both ridiculous and impractical, but not the end of the world.

At this stage, and I assure you that I am maintaining objectivity, there are more pros. As a disclaimer though, your location does have a significant impact.

Advantages and Disadvantages of Single and Multiple Member LLCs

For a Single-Member LLC, it's a one-person show – that's you, in charge of everything! Your LLC is like its own cool entity, doing its thing independently. Now, onto the Multi-Member LLC vibe – this one's a group effort. Got two or more buddies sharing the steering wheel, making decisions together for the company's ride.

I don't need to expand much on the single/multiple terms, so it should suffice to say that some LLCs have a single member, and others have multiple members, to state the obvious. Let's look at the ramifications of both, focusing on advantages vs disadvantages.

The primary advantage, whether a single or multiple LLC is control. As a single member, you have complete control, as it is you, you, and you; that goes without saying. In a multi member LLC, control doesn't have to be guided by investment, number of votes, or by any form of hierarchical system of management. Remuneration and profit share are not subject to the stringent regulations applied to corporations.

Again, tax processes are quite simple, and every member is seen by the tax man as self-employed. Thus, the entity does not turn in corporate tax assessments, rather, the members do their own individual returns.

Personally, I feel more in control, being seen as self-employed by the state, but this can be a double-edged corporate sword when it comes to single or multiple members.

Single member means complete control and decision making. Multi-member could lead to disagreements, in terms of what to declare, or how expenses are run through the LLC. So that can be a disadvantage, but then again, as a member, you are not forced to disclose how you structure your returns.

Also bear in mind that in any business relationship, there will be all sorts of disagreements, not related to tax, so the disadvantages can be quite broad.

I have been in management positions in the past, but I found that my non-confrontational personality made it difficult to be assertive enough. So, I'd rather be a single member LLC, to maintain autonomy.

What I am trying to say is that actual business acumen isn't always the factor that these decisions turn on, and everybody always says not to make business decisions based on emotion. I agree and I don't, but you need to analyze your personality. You may favor paying more taxes and having autonomy than paying less taxes but risking professional differences, leading to toxic business relationships.

A slightly different advantage is that non-citizens can form LLCs, which is certainly not the case all over the world. Although I would argue that this is a good thing, the 'out of the box' issue could be xenophobia, but that isn't related to limiting one's liability, and I don't want to get into pseudo-politics.

The biggest disadvantage is issuing stocks to outside investors, which is prohibited by law in LLCs, and that would be a 'do not pass go' scenario.

One of my former companies was a commodity trading LLC, that owned nothing, not even a mobile phone, and that was from a solely personal asset protection point of view. It worked well, because I was your antithetical middleman. I bought salt and rice from suppliers and delivered them to customers on flat-bed vehicles without even seeing a truck or the product.

As Bob Dylan said, in his 1978 single, 'Like a Rolling Stone,' *"When you ain't got nothing, you got nothing to lose."* To me, protecting myself, in my personal capacity, is the most important thing, generally, and in business. Thus, I see it as a very advantageous convention of an LLC. However, I have met people that thrive on risk, and can become addicted to the thrill of risk-taking. I kind of understand that, but I'd rather go skydiving than put my personal financial comfort on the line.

Should You Form an LLC?

It's too early to say. I encourage you to read on, but you should have a rudimentary understanding of LLCs at this juncture; however, I do implore you to get as much information as you can before deciding.

It can be compared to rushing into a romantic relationship. Early on you think that you have met your person, but as time goes by, you realize that you have made a big mistake and that the two of you are incapable of functioning as a happy couple. When you look back, you come to terms with the fact that you should have taken things slowly in the beginning. You regret that you jumped straight in before finding out whether the person's traits, habits, and disposition were compatible with you as an individual.

So, get the info, assess the viability, and make your business decision based on as much knowledge as you can gain. Read other books and articles or find YouTube videos that can help you and dispel some fears that you may have.

Don't be too hard on yourself or put excess amounts of pressure on your decisions, just avoid rushing.

Chapter Summary

Limit personal liability, or LLCs, means that a member or members' personal assets and investments are not the property of your company.

This scenario reflects the intent of the legislation, and as we have seen, legal protection is vital in any sense, but specifically when it comes to separating your LLC from yourself (or other members).

Taxation can be managed in a simple way, members are treated like self-employed individuals, and deal with the IRS as such.

To stick my neck out there, single member LLCs are not that different from multiple member LLCs, but there is the risk of disagreements.

Unlike corporations, investment, dividends, and general operation of the LLC is simpler and not subject to the strict corporate bureaucracy and regulations.

Lastly, 'knowledge' yourself up instead of making a snap decision, or an ill-informed one. Decisions about your financial future are not flippant, so, take your time and keep it as simple as possible!

CHAPTER 2
IS IT RIGHT FOR YOUR BUSINESS?

The only way of finding out if an LLC is your best business vehicle is to look at other types of entities in a similar way to Chapter One—compare the intricacies of different structures, tax, functionality, and personal protection, to make an informed decision.

Don't lose sight of the fact that within the realm of LLCs, there are what I would loosely term, 'sub-categories' that do differ, but for now, it is time for corporation information.

Corporations Explored

Most people have heard of John Rockefeller, the Oil magnate, and to a lesser extent, Andrew Carnegie, one of the pioneers of the industrial development of steel manufacture. These two men were important influencers on major corporation operation and the development thereof.

As an interesting fact, corporations in the U.S. became a 'thing' in the 1790's, but the Boston Manufacturing Company became the first corporation with large reach and influence when it was formed in 1813. So, corporations have been around for over 200 years, and are over 150 years older than LLCs… but older doesn't mean better.

I remain objective, so it is time to unpack the ins and outs of corporations by addressing the three main points relating to formation, operation, and individual life span.

The Structure of Corporations

When I say structure, I am using quite a broad-brush stroke that encompasses actual legal structure, but also structure in a practical and operational sense.

First off, corporations have shareholders, as opposed to members, like LLCs. The shareholders are the owners of a corporation, and ownership is determined by the number of shares held. For example, if a corporation has 100 shares, and you own 30 shares, your percentage shareholding is 30%. If you own 50 shares, your percentage shareholding is 50%, and so on.

I talked about my trading business a bit earlier and stated that it was an LLC that had no outside investors. It is not impossible to find outside investors, but it does come with its own set of risks in LLC scenarios.

Corporations are financial entities that attract outside investors. One of the reasons being that shareholding allocation, records and transfer follow a standard set of rules, which create eternal life for any corporation.

Remember that LLCs can cease to exist as I explored in Chapter One, and depending on your business goals, may lead you to favor a corporation over an LLC, or vice versa.

Requirements in the day-to-day running of corporations follow stringent rules, and it can feel like there are a lot of processes that can delay decision making, but if everyone pulls together and effectively follows the rules, then the processes can operate hastily. This is somewhat rare though.

Every important decision must be overseen by the board of directors, which is a compulsory tenet of a corporation. This type of oversight is a good thing when it comes to a thorough assessment of what is best for the corporation. The bad part is that it is often difficult to get all the directors into one room to have these types of discussions, hence the delays as mentioned above.

Annual financials must, by law, be drawn up and presented. This can be complicated and the bigger the corporation, the bigger the complication, which most often means outside auditors, who don't come cheap. If you are like me, and prefer feeling that you have complete control, a corporation probably will not work for you.

Taxation, when it comes to corporations, is more complicated and cynics refer to 'double taxation,' meaning that the corporation is taxed on profits, and shareholders are taxed on dividends.

To some, it makes sense, to others, it is just the IRS taking the mickey. I will explore this factor in detail in Chapter Eight, but I think it is safe to say that NOBODY wants to get the run-around by the IRS.

I must again remind you of my objectivity, but for arguments sake, let's say you are favoring LLCs at this point—then you need to gain some knowledge. Here we go!

Different Types of LLCs

Now that you have an understanding of corporations and how they differ from LLCs, let's change focus to the differences between different LLCs.

Certain types of LLCs do overlap, but still maintain legal separation between member and company. Hence the taxation as an individual.

You already know what single member and multiple member LLCs are and how they operate, broadly speaking, so on we go to the other types. Before I get there, I must mention that not all states recognize every type of LLC, but you can register most types of LLCs in most states.

Member-Managed LLC

I'm not a fan of the term 'one-man-band,' but it is appropriate in this case. If your business is small, you probably want to manage and run it on your own. In any case, if you are just getting your business going, you don't want to be wasting part of your initial start-up and running costs.

You will wear many hats—coffee maker, accountant, repair person, sales expert, and many more. The moral is, just do it… yourself. Be cautious though, don't keep banging your head against the wall, trying to do things out of your scope.

Also consider that if your LLC becomes highly successful very quickly, you probably won't be able to do everything yourself; in which case, help is available, it is just about finding the right person for the job.

Manager-Managed LLC

Let's take the example of a food outlet or restaurant. You absolutely have to have staff, and I haven't come across too many restaurants that are owner-member managed, although there are some around. I guess your smaller, boutique type restaurants, or outlets that only serve breakfast and lunch, can be owner managed.

If your restaurant is open from 8 a.m. to 10 p.m. though, and you member-manage, soon you will become exhausted, but if you appoint a competent manager, you can focus on the areas of the business that require your attention as a single member.

A quick tip, when you hire a manager, or any staff member for that matter, you need to be thorough, from paying attention to the resume to contacting previous employers, to discuss the potential employee's references. The interview is also important, and that human connection is too. If you are uncomfortable in any way with a potential manager, then carry on looking.

Domestic LLC

This refers to an LLC in a particular state, and you could say that the LLC 'lives' in XYZ-state. So, XYZ-state is then said to be the 'domicile' or residence, being the legal terms for your LLC's home, so to speak.

Just a quick reminder that an LLC is a person, i.e., a juristic one, and its members are natural persons. The term "juristic person" refers to a legal entity that is recognized as having certain rights and responsibilities similar to those of a natural person (an individual).

So, when I say that "an LLC is a person, i.e., a juristic one," it means that, in the eyes of the law, an LLC is considered a distinct entity with legal rights and obligations. However, these terms aren't rigid; they are legal concepts subject to interpretation.

Foreign LLC

Not all LLCs operate in one state only, and may have offices or factories in various states, alternatively they may just generate income from deals concluded in other states. This is an example of an overlap because this type of LLC is registered as domestic in one state and foreign in the others, in which it conducts business.

Professional Limited Liability Company

If you are a professional license holder, such as a doctor or an accountant, you are pretty much restricted to this type of LLC, whether it is single or multiple members—so another small overlap.

You may elect to be regarded as an S Corporation for tax effective purposes to minimize self-employment tax burdens. I will delve into taxation in more depth later in this book; it is important!

Series LLCs

I would say that this is my least favorite type of LLC, and there are a good few states that agree with me. My thinking is that if you want to make your entity an LLC, for simplicity, then Series won't work for you.

You have an umbrella LLC, with other LLCs below it, operating completely separately, in terms of rights, obligations, debts, and taxation. I guess I am being a little subjective here, but again, the choice is yours, I am just giving opinions and information.

What to Consider When Choosing a Type of LLC

A lot of successful business people will tell you that they went by their gut, or that they followed a hunch, in making a vital decision. That is all good and well, but I would apply these 'sixth sense type' emotions to a deal, or an idea to find a new niche. Choosing the right way to do those things, in terms of your entity type, should be a more measured consideration.

There are a fair number of factors that can guide your decision to choose the LLC that works best for you.

Number of Members

I don't want to repeat myself too much, but I do need to in order to ensure that you are reminded of all elements. This is very important.

Single LLC members enjoy legal protection in their personal capacities and are taxed as an individual… so are multiple members though, thus the choice here would be directed towards your venture, in a personal sense.

Whether there is one member or a gazillion, each member is taxed as an individual.

Everyday Functions of Members

The choice here is member-management or manager-management and would depend on your availability and start-up capital. Maybe you have investment properties and draw a significant income there from, so you can invest a large sum in a new LLC and can afford a manager from day one. On the other hand, if you have limited funds and have to save every which way you can, then your natural choice would be member-management.

Sometimes the choice isn't easy, and you may have to relinquish a bit of immediate control for the financial growth of your LLC. There are of course systems that you can put in place to monitor a manager's performance, which is important in any employer/employee scenario.

Should You Register Your LLC as Domestic or Foreign?

If you intend on creating a multi-state LLC then foreign is your option, but don't forget that it will be domestic to the initial state. This factor depends entirely on the type of business: If you open a restaurant in one state, and have no interest in creating a chain, or even opening independent restaurants in other states, then a domestic LLC is perfect for you. If your goal is to have restaurants in multiple states, then a foreign LLC is more suited to you.

Are the Members Licensed Professionals?

There are many careers that require a professional license, and you will, of course, know that you have that license, depending on your field of expertise. So, this is quite a simple one when it comes to choosing the best LLC, which in this scenario would be a Professional Limited Liability Company.

With professional licenses comes the risk of being sued for malpractice, but if there are multiple members in these types of LLCs, only the member being sued for malpractice can attract liability. To put it more simply, if you require a professional license you have to form a PLLC (if you want to steer away from a corporation, which is probably your best bet as a professional).

Take note that if you have changed vocations, and even though you have a professional license, you are no longer operating in that field, then you are unable to form an PLLC. For example, a former doctor starts a furniture manufacturing business. No license is required, so a PLCC no longer applies. Basically, that option is no longer there, and perhaps makes the decision an easier one.

Is the Point of the LLC to Create Multiple Opportunities?

This choice can be made using two examples that are suited to series LLCs, and you could even treat the term 'series' as one that also means multiple... sort of.

Multiple Restaurants

To put it very simply, let's say someone chokes on a bone in one of your restaurants, your other two restaurants cannot be held liable. It might sound obvious, and no offense to the legislators, but the law really has left the door open wide for ridiculous suits.

Rental Properties

You own three apartment complex properties. If there is an air conditioner in one of the units, and it falls on your tenant and they get injured, your other two properties attract zero liability. Again, sounds obvious, but the things people litigate over leaves one aghast from time to time.

Chapter Summary

Corporations differ from LLCs in that they have a stricter framework and set of rules.

LLCs have members, whereas corporations have shareholders who are seen as the owners of whatever corporation it may be. That percentage ownership is dependent on how many shares each owner holds (50% share = 50% ownership).

Corporations have directors, and decision making is subject to board of director meetings. This extra oversight does make sense because most often corporations are largely funded by investors, who entrust the board to make the correct decisions.

On the accounting side, annual financials have to be produced, which can be complicated and require outside, independent auditors.

In terms of LLCs specifically, your circumstances will dictate whether you will be a single member or a multi member. If you have restricted capital and choose to be a single member, your LLC will be member managed. The same applies to multiple members, and an option if you are flexible in terms of capital, you may want to appoint a manager.

If you want to operate in one state, then you will favor a domestic LLC, and if your business is run in multiple states, you will use a foreign LLC.

Professionally licensed individuals are inevitably going to set up Professional Limited Liability Companies.

Series LLCs are suited to multiple opportunity businesses, and the examples I gave were real estate and restaurant ownership, where each entity making up the multiple opportunity LLC is exempt from legal responsibility attached to the other entities.

So, there are the choices, but before we press on, if you have the feeling that you have been bombarded with too much information, I recommend flicking through this chapter and Chapter One again to make notes and consolidate your understanding.

CHAPTER 3
STARTING AN LLC

I am not one for administration or for reading instructions properly. You can imagine how I approach putting together an Ikea table.

These traits are not good when it comes to starting a business entity, so my recommendation is to take the required steps slowly, and don't start thinking that you know what to do before you know how to do it. It's kind of like saying, "Make sure that you read the instructions."

The Seven Steps

Step One: Choosing a Name

This is important for many reasons, and the first obvious one is that you need to have the kind of name that will get your business noticed.

From a purely personal perspective, I would avoid names like, "Gloves 4 U," or "Guitars 'R Us." They sound cheesy and are definitely overused; but in their defense, you know what you are going to get.

There are lots of considerations, and I would urge you to write down and ponder over some options before you check if there are existing LLCs with the name that you are set on.

Avoid anything controversial and don't use profanity in the title. Don't have any sexual, political, or religious connotations to your name. I once saw a company called, "Trust in God Trucking," and I will admit that it does have a ring to it, but please always respect people with different beliefs. Additionally, you might also limit your ability to work with them. You don't want a name that is difficult to pronounce, as you don't want potential customers saying, "Pardon? Could you please say that again?"

Get onto Google and look at businesses similar to yours, see what kind of names they use, and get a guideline.

Shortly after I left college, I very stupidly started an LLC called BC Sourcing and Distribution. The name does not tell you what the business does, and it's awkward to say. However, in certain circumstances, you may want this to be the situation. I could have decided to go into industry, and call my LLC, BG Precision Window Glazing; easy to say, easy to remember, no doubt about what service the company provides.

There can also be personal influences involved. For instance, there is a company called "Bud's Biscuits" in an industrial area close to where I live. The owner's first family dog was named "Bud" and fits the title well.

I have not yet mentioned registering a 'Doing Business As,' called a DBA for short, so let's get to it.

Whether you have a single member LLC, or are a member of a multiple member LLC, you may want to avoid using your name or the names of your fellow members as part of your business name.

As an aside, but also as an explanation, in certain countries you can buy off the shelf companies, and form a 'trading as' entity. So, the name of the shelf company may be, "A and S Services" for instance, but you are a plumbing business, so you could call the business, "Mark Wright Tip Top Plumbing." The full name will be, "A and S Services, trading as, Mark Wright Tip Top Plumbing," but you are only required to use "Mark Wright Tip Top Plumbing" on your signage, company docs, business cards, etc.

People actually make money out of registering companies with common names that businesses may require. The company doesn't actually trade, but if you want to use that specific name, you can buy the shelf company—but you are essentially buying the name.

You can look at the DBA registration as an opposite of the Mark Wright scenario. You want to maintain anonymity as far as possible, whereas Mark wants his name out there in the public. When registering a DBA, you can quite literally make up any name, as long as it is not yet taken, which is a good idea, especially if your industry niche is extremely specific and there is significant risk involved.

What I am getting at is that by registering a DBA, you do not have to use your name or the names of your fellow members on signage, letterheads, and the like. You could go with, "Onboard Enterprizes," or "PG Management," or whatever else suits your fancy.

Step Two: Appointing a Registered Agent

A registered agent is the person who receives legal and/or financial documents and notices on behalf of the LLC and passes such onto the person or people in charge.

You can appoint yourself, another member of the LLC, an employee, or your auditors if the appointee is available during business hours in the state where your LLC is registered.

A company, such as a law firm or accounting firm, can be registered as an agent, which is only necessary if your LLC expands quickly.

The appointment of a company requires an annual fee, different in every state, but not more than a couple hundred dollars annually.

Step Three: Obtaining the Articles of Organization Form

These forms are referred to by different names in different states, so don't be afraid to call the form the wrong thing. That is a very small issue. You can find the form on your state authorities' website and download it for completion, before returning it by way of upload, email, or hand delivery.

Step Four: Preparing the Articles of Association Form

The information required is your name if you are a single member, otherwise all the names of members in a multi-member LLC, their places of residence, and the principal business address.

You will also need to complete a section detailing the purpose of the business, how it will be managed, and the intended duration of operation.

Lastly, the registered agent's details are required, from which point you can submit the form to your state authority.

In certain states you need to publish a notice stating that you will be registering an LLC. This must obviously be done prior to completing the articles of organization form.

Below is a basic example of a simple articles of association:

ARTICLES OF INCORPORATION OF:

XYZ GARBAGE REMOVALS (LLC)

Under the business corporation laws of ABC state, the following information required is both true and correct.

The name of the LLC is XYZ Garbage Removals.

The principal place of incorporation is

_____

The names and addresses of the members are

_____

The name and address of the registered agent is

_____

The purpose of the incorporation of the LLC is

_____

The management structure of the LLC is

_____

The period of duration of the LLC is

_____

_____   _____

Member one signature   Member two signature

_____

Witness signature

_____

Date

Step Five: Filing the Articles of Association Form

When you file the form, no matter the method, you will be required to pay a filing fee; the amount of which is state dependent.

You will then be issued with a registration certificate, which is the documents that banks will need you to produce, so that the LLC can open a business bank account.

When obtaining a tax number, the registered certificate is needed, so make a few copies, have them certified, and keep them in a safe place.

Future customers or suppliers may request to see the certificate before entering into credit agreements, so don't think that you will never need it after registration of your LLC.

Step Six: The Operating Agreement

This agreement should be very specific, even more so if you are creating a multiple member LLC. Think of it like the rules to a game or sport, you must follow them. They are not compulsory in every state, but I would advise any LLC to create one anyway.

Look at it like a business plan that you would present, so include specifics as to operational management, capital investment, and profit share. Also use the agreement to define roles and procedures for effective day-to-day running.

Even if it is a single member LLC, you have to have a plan, or at the very least, a framework around which your plan is built. An accountant or an attorney could assist you in drawing up the agreement, but there are a plethora of templates that you can find on the internet, if you would like to do it yourself.

Step Seven: Keep Your LLC Alive

Take note of the requirements in your state, some LLCs have to pay renewal fees every year, others pay bi-annually. Some states require reports, others don't.

If changes are made to your LLC, you need to inform the state authority. It would be a disaster if you lost a big supply contract, for instance, because you forgot to tick a small box.

Treat your business like a person, and do the things needed to keep that person happy, healthy, and functional.

Before I turn to business-friendly states that you should consider when registering your LLC, I would like to address, and give some tips on, something that will likely prove vital in the setting up and early trading stages of your LLC... the money.

Business Finance For Your LLC

If you are in a position to start your LLC without needing finance then you are doing well. However, it is more common for people to have to take out some sort of loan to finance the set-up of their business. The idea of borrowing money and having to pay a bank back over an extended period can be a scary one, but you probably haven't realized that there are several options out there, and some can even be tailored specifically to your needs.

I would like to take you through each option, followed by advice on what to look out for in terms of wasting money. If you spend smart then you can pay off your loan sooner. One quick tip before we get started: If you take out a term loan, meaning a loan that is paid back over a certain term, 24 months for instance, paying a little more than the set installment every month will have a significant reduction on the interest.

Start-up Loan

If you are setting up a new LLC, as opposed to converting an existing business into an LLC, then you will qualify for a start-up loan. This type of finance is often accompanied by reasonable interest rates because of the fact that it takes time to establish cash flow. Unless you have a product that sells almost immediately it will take time to build your turnover and become profitable. A start-up loan is also often over a generous period of time, meaning that the installments are quite low.

Small Business Loan

A small business loan is structured in the same way as a start-up loan and can be accessed by new businesses. However, the start-up loan option is always the recommended one because the terms are generally more favorable. Because a start-up loan cannot be accessed by an existing business that is being converted into an LLC, a small business loan is your only other option in this class of finance. It operates in the same way, i.e., an amount of money is lent to your LLC, to be paid back over a certain number of months at a specified interest rate.

Advantages of Start-up and Business Loans

Other than the reasonable terms of the start-up loan, both give you finite terms, repayment amounts, and interest rates from the outset. Thus, you can plan as best possible to have the payment amount in your LLCs account by the monthly due date.

Business Cash Advance

This type of loan is not ideal for a start-up, but there is nothing stopping your LLC from using this finance vehicle. It does come with high risk, because the amount that your LLC qualifies for is based on turnover and profit projections. You will have to formalize your projections, which is easier if you are already in business. A typical scenario would be if your LLC has been operational for a year and you have taken on a project that requires relatively immediate expenditure in order to receive a profitable return in three months from applying for the cash advance. You would then have to present the bank with your required expenditure, and projections of income based on contracts that you will secure as a result of the said expenditure. The terms of a cash advance may be negotiable contingent on when your LLC will be in a position to repay the advance.

Accounts Receivable Financing

This method is most common in businesses that operate 30-day accounts. If you are starting a brand new LLC, you must remember that just because your debtors sign credit agreements undertaking to pay your accounts on a 30-day basis, there is no real guarantee that it could slip to 35 or even 45 days. Your LLC will suffer the knock-on effect, in that without income from your debtors you cannot pay your creditors.

Accounts receivable finance is a solution, whereby you present your issued invoices to the bank and they pay your LLC minus a fee. When your debtors pay their accounts, the money is used to pay the bank back. It isn't advisable to use this type of finance, but sometimes it is inevitable, and if well-managed there won't be a problem.

Imagine you've just launched an LLC that provides consulting services to various clients. Your business operates on a 30-day payment term, meaning your clients are expected to settle their invoices within 30 days of receiving your services.

Now, as a new LLC owner, you quickly realize that despite having clear credit agreements with your clients for a 30-day payment cycle, there's always a risk of delays. Some clients might extend the payment period to 35 or even 45 days, impacting your LLC's cash flow. This delay, in turn, affects your ability to meet financial obligations to your suppliers and creditors.

In such a scenario, you might opt for Accounts Receivable Financing. You approach a bank and present the invoices you've issued to your clients. The bank, recognizing the value of these invoices, agrees to advance a certain percentage of the total amount to your LLC, deducting a fee for its services.

As your clients eventually settle their accounts within the agreed-upon timeframe, the funds received are used to repay the bank. While Accounts Receivable Financing is not always the ideal financial strategy, especially due to associated fees, it becomes a pragmatic solution in situations where delays in payment are unavoidable. If managed effectively, this financial approach ensures your LLC can navigate cash flow challenges without compromising its operational stability.

Short-term Loan

In a private person context these loans are referred to as 'payday loans' and are issued to applicants who have run out of money a week or a few days prior to receiving their monthly salary. The loan is advanced to the individual and is paid back the day that they get their salary. Very convenient, but the interest rates are outrageous, as this finance can be out of desperation.

When it comes to your LLC, you may need access to cash to allow you to pay your staff on time because one of your debtors is late paying your account. The same principle applies: the bank advances you a sum, which you use to cover your wage bill, and when your late debtor makes payment, then you repay the bank, also at a large interest rate.

Business Line Credit Option

The vital term here is 'option' because you only use the available credit when you need to. The option is there, and you can make use of it if you want to. This finance is advisable in that banks will often have interest free periods. For instance, if you exercise the option and use $5,000 dollars and manage to pay it back within 21 days then it attracts no interest. You may be wondering how this is beneficial to the bank and the answer would be that it isn't. However, there are enough businesses out there that are unable to make the repayments within the interest free period, to keep the bank in credit.

Movable Equipment Financing

If you need to buy an industrial printer for your LLC, you can use the printer as collateral. The bank will advance you the money, which you will use to purchase the printer. Your LLC is required to make repayments every month, but if a payment is missed then the bank can repossess your printer. You need to see this from a long term perspective because if the loan is over a 24 month period, when you finish paying the printer off it is then the sole property of your LLC.

Any form or credit is a grudge 'purchase'. You do not want to pay interest but in order to get the equipment that you need, a loan is the only option, which means that interest is inevitable. The risk in this case is not being able to meet your repayments and thus having your printer repossessed. Unfortunately business comes with risk, so there is no way around it in some instances.

Commercial Mortgage for Immovable Property

This idea is contradictory to the limited liability concept, because the premise is that an LLC that owns no assets or very few, offers personal protection. However, purchasing immovable property may advance your LLC. In the case of a storage warehouse, it may be more economical to buy a warehouse as opposed to renting one. If your LLC is in this situation and the plan is to purchase a warehouse because when it is paid off, profits will naturally increase, due to not having repayment commitments. If your LLC rents on an indefinite basis, the rental expense will always be there. It comes down to the risk factor and the probable longevity of your LLC.

Let's take the warehouse example further. You decide that it is financially viable to buy instead of renting. Contrary to popular belief when you take out a commercial mortgage, your LLC owns the warehouse. Many people think, and the same goes for mortgages over homes, that the bank 'owns' the house, and if you fail to make your payments, the bank takes the house back.

Actually a mortgage is a personal loan that you use to purchase property and that property becomes collateral for the loan. Thus, if you fail to make the payments then the bank will foreclose, meaning that it will sell the warehouse, in this case and use the proceeds to settle the loan.

Most often a public auction is held and the money paid for the warehouse is then credited to the loan. Usually the warehouse sells for less than its value and there will be a shortfall, which your LLC will have to settle. This is where the limited liability kicks in. If your LLC has no other assets that can be liquidated to settle the shortfall, also called the arrears, then you and your fellow members are safe from personal liability. Essentially you need to crunch the numbers and assess viability. If you look at it from a different perspective and hypothetically you fail to make rental payments, then you will get kicked out, and the owner or company that owns the warehouse will have no recourse against you personally.

Small Business Administration Loan

This type of finance is partially backed by the government, which doesn't actually provide the money, but rather stands as a guarantor for the repayment of part of the loan.

The Dangers of Credit

It may not be necessary to state but you need to spend wisely, especially when you are starting out. Whatever type of finance you opt for will see a cash injection into your LLCs account. If there is a surplus after you have bought the equipment that you took the loan to buy, it is tempting to spend that money on top of the range furniture, for instance. That would be financially irresponsible, but many people fall into that trap. Be careful and use common sense.

Can you imagine getting all your documents together and going from bank to bank to finance house and back until you find the right institution offering the type of finance best suited to your LLC; it would take up way too much time that could otherwise be dedicated to setting up. There is an excellent tool that can be used to minimize that potential time loss to something minimal. It is called a business lending marketplace.

Business Lending Marketplace

A business lending marketplace is a one-stop shop website where you plug in all the details of your LLC and hit search. The results are abundant and allow you to compare different types of finance options. You will also be able to see all the information about how the loan/s operates, what the repayment periods and interest rates are, as well as any fees involved. The obvious advantage is timesaving, but there are other advantages as follows:

Flexibility

Flexibility is a key factor when it comes to finding the right financing for your LLC, and Lendio.com stands out as my preferred business marketplace. The platform's user-friendly interface, extensive reach, and prompt results make the financing process seamless. Lendio.com collaborates with more than 75 lenders, providing you with a diverse range of finance options tailored to the unique needs of your LLC. Whether you're seeking a start-up loan, a commercial mortgage, or a small-business loan, Lendio.com offers the flexibility to discover the finance solution that aligns perfectly with your business goals.

Amount and Time Period

Due to the multiple options, you can find available loans from small to large. The latter takes more time to apply for, but an urgent loan for a small amount, used in emergencies, is available within 24 hours (generally). Make sure you have the means or will have the means to pay it back so you don't have to pawn your tv.

Assistance from Experts

You can have real-time conversations with people, not bots, that are trained in finance and can give you advice and recommendations. When dealing with them, don't think that any question is a stupid question. They have heard it all. Using a business lending marketplace is, without a doubt, your best option.

Which State(s) to File Your Operating Agreement in

Interestingly, you can set up your LLC in a state from which it does not operate. Having said that, it is much more effective to register your LLC in the state in which you live.

Either way, you will have to file requisite paperwork, tax returns, and the like in your home state, so think of the practicality before you register; however, don't discount financial effectiveness when registering your LLC out of state.

Filing in Your Home State

This is based on convenience. You are more than likely familiar with the laws and regulations in your state, the different governmental branches and their location, as well as contacts that can advise and assist.

Consider the physical site of your business and where most of the trading is done. If the answer to these two considerations is the state that you live in, then practicality dictates filing in that state.

If your business operates in more than one state, it will have to be registered as a domestic LLC and a foreign LLC. These days, remote work is so common that this type of registration has become more popular. There is always the cost factor though. If you register in a foreign state, you will either have to travel there regularly in the set-up process or appoint a representative to do it for you.

Once more, it depends on your individual business circumstances.

Filing in a Foreign State

I am obviously aware that readers are likely to live all over the country, so I will look at three states in which to register an LLC, but you can investigate your home state regulations at the correct department.

The reason for looking at the following three states is due to their business friendliness, tax implications, and simplicity of structure.

Delaware

This state is very popular when registering a foreign LLC, largely because it has a reputation for being business-friendly, and that is vital if you are not going to be present.

Another reason is the Chancery Court, dedicated to business disputes only, which lends itself to streamlining matters and reaching faster resolution, than in a general court.

In addition, judges on the bench in the Chancery Court are experts in business, compared to judges in general courts, as they sit in a variety of different matters, opening themselves up to poor judgments.

Delaware does not tax out-of-state income, so if a large part of your business operations, income, and expenditure fall in a foreign state, your LLC is exempt in Delaware.

Nevada

There is no business income tax in Nevada, nor capital gains or franchise tax, which is no doubt a big advantage, especially for franchised LLCs. There is a small downside, which is the fees, and requirements for obtaining a business license and the annual filing fees. Tax vs fees is the basis for your decision.

I talked about operating agreements and how they often complicate things. In Nevada, they are not required, nor are annual meetings.

If you want to remain anonymous as far as possible, then take note of the fact that Nevada does not have an information sharing agreement with the IRS. To me, the IRS must stay out of your activities, other than actual tax related matters.

Wyoming

Wyoming is catching up to Delaware as a business-friendly state. There is no business or franchise tax, and processes are becoming more streamlined.

A convention in Wyoming when it comes to LLCs is something called lifetime proxy, which means that you, as a single member, or you and your partners, as a multiple member LLC, can appoint a representative to handle the administrative affairs.

This approach would work if you have other business operations, or if you don't have time to do justice to your participation. Total anonymity is the major benefit here, but that becomes irrelevant if you don't have a problem with, let's say, being visible.

States that are Disadvantageous to Register Your LLC

The worst of the worst is New Jersey because taxes are high, percentage wise, but also because there are virtually no tax breaks. Even setting up your LLC is expensive, so this is one to avoid.

In California, individual and corporate tax are not pocket friendly considering that the unemployment rate and general cost of living are substantially higher than in other states.

It basically comes down to cost and viability, which go hand in hand. New York for instance isn't LLC tax friendly, and the set-up costs are high.

Minnesota, Ohio, and Maryland are all high tax states when it comes to LLCs, and there are many more that are way less favorable than Delaware, Nevada, and Wyoming.

You will need to do some research on this one. The different regulatory bodies in each state are obliged to provide you with cost and tax information, so that may be a good start.

Do I Need a Lawyer to Register my LLC?

It is not a legal requirement that a lawyer attend to the registration, but it is not a bad option if you can find a lawyer with the right expertise.

My advice would be to avoid this route, as lawyers have been known to charge as much as $5,000 for this service, which to me is absolutely ridiculous! I am not saying that every lawyer charges that much, but I would not pay such outrageous fees for something I can do myself.

This book is designed to help you understand the processes, and generally the relevant state departments are very helpful, especially if you can show that you have tried to educate yourself on LLCs.

My advice would be to book a consultation with a business lawyer, hear what that person has to say, and then make a call.

A lawyer may be needed at a later stage, if your LLC grows quickly, and there are labor or litigation issues, or anything else that you feel you don't have the expertise to handle yourself.

Short answer: don't hire a lawyer unless you have to.

Chapter Summary

Once you decide on a name, you need to make a call as to whether you want to appoint an agent, but for these purposes let's say that you are setting up the LLC on your own.

Get the requisite forms from the specific state authority, fill in all details. Look at it like a business plan. When you are done, make several copies, then file the forms.

The extra copies will come in handy when you need to open a bank account, deal with tax or franchise agreements, amongst others.

It is advisable to draft an operating agreement, detailing the functional running of your LLC. Make sure you are aware of any annual submission requirements and fulfill them when the time comes.

Look at the benefits of registering your LLC in a foreign state, be they simplicity, tax efficacy, or anonymity. Do some investigating into states other than the three in this chapter, to help make your mind up.

Finally, avoid lawyers or other representatives; this book should arm you with the knowledge to proceed on your own. When I say avoid, I don't mean when you really need assistance, but avoid as much as possible if you are confident in your own abilities.

CHAPTER 4
COMMON PITFALLS WHEN STARTING AN LLC

It is vital to know and identify the good and the bad in order to follow the good and avoid the bad. Don't get too discouraged, these pitfalls, as the title suggests, happen often. So all you need to do is understand what they are and steer away from them.

Keep in mind that the sailing won't always be smooth, things will go wrong, that's just life, but if you can prepare for them, then you are on the right track.

I will go into S-Corps in this chapter, which are not actually LLCs, but for good reason. I will also delve deeper into taxation and thresholds.

Six Very Common Pitfalls

Choosing the Wrong Entity

Single member LLCs provide an easy set up. There aren't piles of paperwork, taxation is simple, and your personal liability is completely protected.

Tax wise, you will need to file quarterly returns, but are taxed as an individual on profits. You do have the option of requesting the IRS to tax you as an S-Corp, but why would you do that? To save tax, of course!

If your LLC makes an annual profit of $80,000 USD or more, the taxation as an S-Corp makes sense. You will have to adhere to stricter rules and regulations, such as paying yourself a salary, so you can structure your LLC in the most tax effective manner.

If your LLC is turning an annual profit of $20,000 USD, it would be a very bad decision to ask the IRS to tax you as an S-Corp, because you will end up paying more tax than if you were taxed as an individual.

This is something that you may want to take some additional financial advice on before committing.

Choosing the Wrong State in Which to Register

I referred to Delaware, Nevada, and Wyoming as business-friendly states for several reasons, but largely legal and taxation based. Now, for single member LLCs, or even multiple member LLCs, incorporating a small business may not be worth the trouble.

The inconvenience may not be worth the tax savings and remember that you have to have a representative in the foreign state. That representative's fees may negate the benefits, so a large LLC is more likely to explore multi-state registration.

Again, I say this: keep it simple as far as reasonably possible.

Becoming Non-Compliant

Overlooking something, or neglecting to follow proper practices, even if it is something really small, can cast your LLC into non-compliance, which is not good for your reputation or your LLC's pocket.

Compliance differs from state to state, but the four fundamentals are as follows:

Use your business name in all documents, with LLC as the suffix in every case. It adds professionalism and credibility.

Let's consider an example for using your business name consistently with "LLC" as the suffix:

Before	After Implementing Consistency
Business Card: ABC Innovations	Business Card: ABC Innovations LLC
Invoice: ABC Innovations	Invoice: ABC Innovations LLC
Email Signature: ABC Innovations	Email Signature: ABC Innovations LLC

By consistently incorporating "LLC" as the suffix in all your business documents, you enhance the professionalism and credibility of your company. This practice not only reflects a commitment to transparency but also instills confidence in clients, partners, and stakeholders, emphasizing the legal structure and reliability of your LLC.

Know what the annual reporting rules are and submit reports in line therewith. If there are any changes to your LLC, such as appointing additional members, you must submit the necessary amendment forms, most often referred to as articles of amendment.

DO NOT mix up business funds and personal funds, you may unintentionally open yourself up to IRS scrutiny.

It is also advisable to plan for future uncertain events, such as the passing of a member in a multiple LLC or sale of the business. A simple agreement recording these types of things is strongly recommended.

Forming an LLC Without the Requisite Licenses

There isn't too much to be said about this one. You should know what business license you require, say a real estate license or license to operate, as a financial planner. Get your ducks in a row on this one, you wouldn't want your business to crumble for such a small lack of compliance.

If you are going into a new line of business, let's say construction, there will be a lot of compliance requirements, and whilst you may not require licenses specifically, you will definitely need to follow safety procedures and have compliance certificates awarded.

Do a bit of homework into what your business requires in this regard, and make sure that you do things correctly.

Not Getting the Correct Legal Assistance

As I have said before, using a lawyer to set up your LLC is not necessary, but if you feel more comfortable appointing a lawyer, then go for it. You are more likely to really need legal assistance after setting up your LLC, depending on the complexities of your business. If you want to request that the IRS tax your LLC as an S-Corp, then a lawyer is recommended.

Peace of mind is so important, in business as in life, and if hiring a lawyer to sort out multiple state registration, tax compliance, and all the paperwork in between, will give you peace of mind, then you have your answer right there.

Using Incorrect Documentation

The internet is a gift and a curse because there are unquantified amounts of standard form documents that you can download. The problem is that you need to get your hands on the correct template or set of forms that you require in a specific situation.

This is quite easy to get around, and more often than not, you can get what you require from the state department's website or physically from the department.

If your LLC expands, then you may require different licenses, labor compliance certificates, or safety standard documents. Make sure you do your homework and never presume that you have downloaded the correct form(s). Rather, do your checks and get that peace of mind; alternatively, get some assistance.

Mistakes to Avoid When Running an LLC

If you are a first-time business owner, you must be aware of things that you perhaps would not otherwise have thought of as an employee. Getting your LLC into debt is a massive mistake made all the time. Take as little money as you can out of your LLC, even if your business gets off to a very lucrative start. The idea is to build up a fund that you can draw from in the hard times, the best example of which is Covid-19. Nobody could have foreseen the pandemic, but it happened.

This doesn't mean that you can't have accounts with your customers, suppliers, and service providers as long as you ensure that your cash flow is sufficient. Do background checks into every person or business that you have dealings with during your set-up phase, and make this a habit from day one. When you do business with a new company or individual in the future, that habit should be ingrained in you.

Don't spend company money unnecessarily. If you have an office, you don't need top of the range furniture if your LLC is just starting up. Make sure that your bookkeeping is on point, and that you have oversight of the business operations, day to day. Avoid saying, "I'll just take it out of petty cash." There have to be systems in place, and even if you are a single member LLC, you have to follow the rules that you set for yourself.

Let's look a little closer at four specific potential mistakes.

Not Having a Deadlock Provision in the Operating Agreement

The legal term for a deadlock provision is an 'Impasse Resolution,' and it addresses, well, a deadlock, when making decisions in multiple member LLCs. Don't worry about the legal name, I will use 'deadlock provision.'

For instance, if a four member LLC requires outside finance, and there are two different financial institutions that could grant credit, the four members will vote. If the votes are deadlocked at 2/2, then there has to be a way of finalizing the decision, and the operating agreement will be called upon in such circumstances.

In the context of a business scenario with a deadlock clause, the provision could be designed to address situations where the members of an LLC reach an impasse in decision-making. In this example, let's consider two members: member one and member two.

The deadlock clause could specify that if a unanimous decision cannot be reached, member two, who possesses superior knowledge and understanding of how financiers operate, may be granted the authority to make the final decision. This provision recognizes that in certain matters, especially those related to financing, having a member with specialized expertise can be crucial.

The rationale behind allowing member two to hold the swing vote is based on efficiency and informed decision-making. By entrusting the final decision to the member with the most relevant knowledge, the LLC ensures that decisions related to financing are made with a deep understanding of the financial landscape. This approach acknowledges the expertise of individual members and seeks to prevent prolonged deadlocks by empowering the most informed member to break the tie.

In essence, the deadlock clause serves as a practical mechanism to navigate decision-making challenges within the LLC, promoting efficiency and leveraging the specialized skills of its members to make well-informed choices, especially in critical areas such as finance.

This applies to any decision whatsoever, and if there is no provision in the agreement, the decision-making process could get ugly and complicated.

The Operating Agreement is Outdated

Laws do change from time to time and may require your LLC to amend its operating agreement. It doesn't mean that your business plan has to be changed, just added to, and may even be subtracted from.

If you are not up to speed with the legal requirements in your state, or in foreign states for that matter, and another company litigates against you for non-compliance, if picked up by the other companies, lawyers may put your LLC in a position of disadvantage. Never forget though, that your personal liability is protected, so in this type of situation, things would be way worse without that protection.

Members Do Not Properly Document LLC Activity

This is very common, often because members want to attend to the running of the LLC. At the end of the day, money making work can seem more important than administration, but maintaining records could save your bacon, for these next few reasons.

Imagine your LLC as a bustling kitchen, with members donning chef hats and aprons, passionately whipping up delectable dishes to satisfy customers. In the midst of this culinary chaos, paperwork tends to get overshadowed by the aroma of sizzling ingredients and the clatter of kitchen utensils.

Now, let's say Chef A and Chef B are so engrossed in creating culinary masterpieces that they forget to properly document their recipes, inventory, and expenses. It's not that they don't understand the importance of record-keeping; it's just that the sizzle of the grill and the joy of creating mouth-watering dishes take precedence.

Here's where the trouble brews. When it's time to analyze profits, track expenses, or even spice things up with new menu items, Chef A and Chef B find themselves in a bind. The lack of proper documentation turns their once-vibrant kitchen into a puzzle of missing ingredients and unclear recipes.

This scenario illustrates a common pitfall where the excitement of the creative process overshadows the administrative side of running an LLC. While the money-making magic happens at the stove, a lack of records can leave a bitter aftertaste when it comes to understanding the financial health of the business. So, just as a well-organized kitchen ensures a smooth culinary experience, meticulous documentation in your LLC can save your bacon when it's time to savor the fruits of your labor.

Keeping Proper Records Offers Greater Legal Protection

If a lawsuit arises, the opposing attorneys will try to discredit your LLC by alleging that record keeping paperwork is not in order. The idea is to then come after your personal assets based on a technicality.

This isn't always the case, and in a situation where your LLC is bankrupt, lawyers probably won't even bother coming after you because you have the protection that is limited liability.

Drafting a Memorandum in Order to Record Percentage Shares

You would not want to think that your ownership percentage is 25%, and later discover that it has not been recorded in writing if a dispute arises with your business partners.

Even if you go into business with your best friend, you should still draw up the memorandum as people can fall out. You are protecting every member by doing the memorandum, so don't neglect to draft it.

Picture this: You and your business partner decide to open a magical bookstore, enchanting readers with stories from distant realms. Your ownership in this literary haven is like a golden key, unlocking the treasures within. Now, imagine that your ownership percentage is like the magical essence fueling the bookstore's enchantment.

In the midst of selecting spellbinding books and brewing potions of creativity, you realize the importance of capturing this magic in writing. So, you decide to draft a Memorandum of Ownership, a parchment that not only records but immortalizes each partner's percentage share in the mystical world of books.

As you and your best friend delve into the whimsical world of entrepreneurship, you understand that even the strongest friendships can face storms. What if, in the midst of a heated disagreement over whether to introduce flying broomsticks or teleportation portals in the bookstore, you discover that your ownership percentage has not been inked into the magical contract?

Here's where the memorandum shines as a protective spell. It's not about expecting discord; it's about ensuring that, even in the most harmonious of magical realms, everyone's ownership is crystal clear. The memorandum becomes the enchanted shield, guarding against misunderstandings and disputes that may arise, transforming potential conflicts into mere gusts of wind in the magical library.

So, whether you're brewing potions or drafting memos, the key is to embrace the magic of clarity. By recording each member's ownership percentage in the sacred Memorandum of Ownership, you're not just protecting yourself; you're weaving a spell that safeguards the harmony and magic of your shared literary adventure.

Defining Management Roles

Again, this should be in writing, so everybody involved has clarity as to what their individual roles are, and in the case of confusion for any reason, the management role documents can be consulted.

Look at it like job descriptions and business policies, written down, filed, but hopefully not needed.

In our magical bookstore venture example, drafting a Memorandum of Ownership became akin to capturing the essence of each owner's share in the enchanting realm of literature. This document served as a protective spell, ensuring clarity in ownership percentages even amidst potential disputes. Similarly, defining Management Role Scrolls adds another layer of magic to our literary adventure. These scrolls act as compasses in times of confusion, providing clarity on each member's specific responsibilities and powers within the bookstore. Both the Memorandum and Management Role Scrolls are written enchantments, safeguarded in a mystical archive, ready to transform potential chaos into organized wizardry whenever needed.

Documenting Contributions and Loans

If there comes a time to take money out of your LLC, and there is no record of what you put in, you may face a big problem. The same would apply to personal loans taken from company funds. Keep these records up to date! But as I have said, avoid touching company funds.

Just to clarify, members can borrow from the LLC against their loan accounts, which would not qualify as mixing business and personal transactions.

Transfer of Assets

If your LLC buys assets, you need to draw up and keep sale agreements so that you can account for what your LLC owns, if need be. This would apply in a bankruptcy situation, for instance, in which you would have to transfer assets to creditors, or sell them, to raise money owed.

Mixing Company Funds with Personal Funds

This is a big no no! You must never use company funds for personal expenses, or vice versa. It just muddies the waters and can lead to disputes between members. Don't do it, not even once.

Just think about the possibility of a good business relationship turning sour because of something like this, which should be easy to control. Absolute necessity may arise, but only in extreme circumstances should you go against this rule.

Note, that members loaning the entity money does not qualify as mixing personal and business funds. Members have loan accounts; this is very normal.

Misuse of Company Funds

Excessive use of company funds for personal expenditure amounts to misuse, as well as mixing company and personal bank accounts. You may remember that earlier I did say that this happens and used the example of the forgetful amongst us, who have to use a personal credit card at a business lunch, then claim the amount back. I'm not talking about that in this case.

I mean taking serious amounts of money out of the LLC to take expensive holidays. Causing financial trouble for your LLC by doing so is not fraud, but it is corporate irresponsibility, and the personal asset protection benefit is the veil that can be lifted upon application to court... BE CAREFUL!

Capitalization of the LLC

Purposeful creation of large debts while maintaining small capital balances and then declaring bankruptcy. The debt creation would probably be to fund a lifestyle of skiing holidays, fancy cars, and irresponsible living... BE CAREFUL.

Fraudulent Behavior

Suppose an LLC is specifically formed to de-fraud other businesses or individuals. Fraudsters, in these instances, will make sure that the LLC does not own a thing and also that they do not own a thing. There is no specific formula or set of rules for piercing the corporate veil. The courts approach each situation individually...Let's make a rule... DON'T COMMIT FRAUD.

Chapter Summary

Record keeping and doing things by the book are the themes in this chapter, and you need to do this to cater for something that may come to light in the future where producing records will settle a dispute.

You need to choose the entity that is most effective, especially in terms of tax, so requesting that the IRIS tax you as a C-Corp isn't wise, unless your turnover is significant enough to create tax benefits.

Legal compliance is obviously vital, and for this reason you don't want to get the wrong legal advice or neglect to apply for the correct licenses.

Record everything in writing so as to avoid disputes and to cover yourself and your LLC in the case of litigation, IRS scrutiny, and day to day running policies.

It may seem a bit overwhelming, but if you break it down step by step, you will be fine.

CHAPTER 5
CONVERTING YOUR EXISTING BUSINESS INTO AN LLC

This may sound like something quite challenging, and it is to a certain extent, but probably not as much as you might think. Perhaps you jumped straight in and just started operating your business as yourself, otherwise referred to as a sole proprietorship, and you have come to realize that an LLC offers you more protection and tax advantages than a sole proprietorship.

Maybe your business has grown significantly, or you have been awarded a big contract, which will increase expenditure (and hopefully profits). Looking into converting that business into an LLC, and once again, limiting your personal liability, would be very viable.

There could be a situation in which converting your business to an LLC may not be viable; however, you will only know that if you explore the options and possibilities, which I will deal with in this chapter.

At this stage of the book, you should have a conceptual understanding of LLCs, so you have an advantage off the bat. Before I continue, I need to mention that conversions are not possible in all states.

What Kind of Businesses Can Be Converted Into LLCs?

The specific entities that can form a new LLC or become members of an existing LLC are sole proprietorships, corporations, and LLC groups, also called parent companies in a conversion sense.

Banks, public financiers, insurance companies, medical protection companies, and several others cannot legally form or be part of LLCs for various reasons, which I am not going to go into. For these purposes they are irrelevant.

Sole Proprietorship

This one is pretty simple, as a sole proprietor is just one person, so for all intents and purposes, a brand-new LLC is formed by following the usual processes.

Articles of organization have to be filed with the relevant state department. The processes are very similar from state to state. I would encourage you to refer to the requirements, as discussed in previous chapters, although I do explore them again in what follows.

Corporation

Articles of organization also have to be filed, but first the corporation must be dissolved. Its assets are said to collapse into the LLC, which can be looked at like a transfer or sale in loose terms. The decision to convert to an LLC is made via shareholder majority vote, which may involve long meetings and discussions.

LLC Groups

This is closer to the sole proprietorship method where existing LLCs became partners in a new LLC, or an LLC that has been newly formed. Articles of organization must be filed in accordance with state laws where the business resides. It may get slightly complicated in multiple state LLC registration, but break it down step by step, use this book, and take outside advice if needed.

Advantages and Disadvantages of Changing Your Business to an LLC

There are advantages and disadvantages to every decision, and they depend on the situation, so I will go through them to allow you to weigh the pros and cons. Practically, pros and cons may differ from person to person, so take note of that. Just because I call it a con, it may have no effect on you or your business, which would make it 'a nothing.'

A couple of things that can slow down processes are directors' meetings and shareholders meetings, which are dispensed with, after conversion to an LLC. Resolutions are also a requirement when making and recording decisions in a corporation, and the rigidity thereof is not present in LLCs.

You will notice a difference in streamlining your business, making faster decisions, and in tax related matters. Converting into an LLC, as I have mentioned, has tax implications, so moving assets into the LLC is seen by the law as a liquidation of those assets, or a sale of those assets. Those two terms are closely related, and the example I am going to give illustrates only the transfer, it has nothing to do with corporations or LLCs.

Let's assume for these purposes that you are a natural person (individual), and you sell your assets to another natural person (individual). This may be by way of a sale agreement or liquidation proceedings, but the moral of the story is that ownership changes.

The corporation is referred to as a juristic person, as is the LLC, so person one (Corp) transfers its assets to person two (LLC), by sale agreement or liquidation, just like the natural person scenario.

Just as tax implications can be an advantage, they can also be a disadvantage in certain scenarios in the asset transfer realm. If the assets are valued quite highly and a 'gain' is made on them, then corporation tax will apply, as well as shareholders tax, so the streamlining that I mentioned earlier may have to be sacrificed in order to save tax.

Tax experts can give great advice on the ramifications of conversions, and how to structure asset transfer to minimize tax. I do recommend this strongly, even if it is a bit costly. Don't be penny wise, but pound foolish.

Procedure to Convert Your Sole Proprietorship to an LLC

This can be fun in a way and exciting, perhaps a new start even! There are six easy steps that can be followed, well not easy, just less complicated.

Confirm the Name of Your Business

There may be an LLC that has the same name as your sole proprietorship, so you need to investigate that through your relevant state authority. If the name is available, great! If not, you will have to come up with a new name.

If you want to be thorough, you should get in touch with the United States Patent and Trademark Office to check that you are not infringing on a trademark. Take note of what I covered in the naming section, found in Chapter Three.

File Articles of Organization

You should remember, as discussed earlier, that this document records the business details, i.e. name, address, contact, purpose of business, member or manager managed etc. If you are using an agent, that person's details must form part of the articles of organization, but an agent is not absolutely necessary, although they can be useful.

Draft Your Operating Agreement

This is not compulsory, but highly advisable to prevent disputes in the future. The agreement is between LLC members, and the idea is for everyone to be clear on operating processes, requirements, and designated roles in the business. Having this agreement in place should make everyone comfortable, know what is expected, and able to proceed confidently.

Tax Compliance

Contact the IRS to check what you need to submit in terms of tax. In a lot of states, the submission will be exactly the same as that required from a sole proprietorship, but it must be done as an LLC. Don't worry, I address tax in more detail in future chapters.

Open a Bank Account

This needs no explanation, but I would say that you should do some investigating into which banks are more viable than others. Charges, administration fees, drawing fees, card fees, and all the other damn fees, differ from bank to bank. There are banks that have tailored accounts for businesses, depending on several factors. The cheapest isn't always the best, so do your research into the financial viability vs the quality of service.

Remember that banks are not going to open an account for an entity or person that lacks credibility, so when you are presenting your business details, you don't want to have your credibility questioned.

Have all information at your disposal, don't use a post office box address, rather have a fixed address. These days everybody uses Google to investigate, so if you have used a random domicile for your LLC, it won't look good in the eyes of the bank.

It is a good idea to set up a website, a very basic one at first, which you can direct the banker who is performing due diligence to, which is a huge step in establishing credibility.

If you can get your LLC to a point where you could do a big launch, get involved in a marketing campaign, or promote your business publicly before you open your bank account, then I am certain that your LLC will not encounter any issues.

Apply for Your Business License

Depending on your industry and state, you may require a business license, so locate the correct authority and fill out the application. If you are unsure, which would be concerning, you should contact the body which has authority of your particular profession.

Procedure to Convert Your Corporation to an LLC

At the risk of getting repetitive, each state is different, but the procedures have a lot of similarities, so here is the general approach.

Create a Conversion Plan

Prepare your conversion plan, including information on current shareholders voting, assets, and meetings of the board of directors, then submit to the correct regulatory authority.

Shareholder Approval is Required

As there may be several shareholders, approval is important and the board will very likely take a vote and produce a resolution, confirming approval (or not). Without approval there is not much that can be done, but shareholders are expected to act measuredly, and delve into all factors before putting the potential conversion to the vote.

File the Correct Documents

I have discussed this extensively, so I won't go into it again, but just remember to get your document ducks in a row, and deliver them to the relevant state authority. It will only be to your advantage.

Procedure to Use Your LLC as a Member of Another LLC

This is referred to as creating a subsidiary LLC, and the set-up process is almost identical to setting up an LLC with multiple natural persons as members. The articles of association must have all the usual details, plus the details of what we call the parent company.

The parent company becomes a member of the new LLC, which can have several parent companies and natural persons as members. Obviously, somebody has to sign on behalf of the parent company, and it is very important to put your designation below your signature. It could be "company owner," "owner/manager," "president," or "executive." The title doesn't matter, but the signature on behalf of the company is the important bit.

Once you have completed the articles of association, I would recommend finding out about what business licenses the parent company and the new LLC require, then make the necessary applications if you have not yet done so.

For your own protection, you can draw up your operating agreement which defines everyone's roles. Make sure that you cross all the 't's' and dot all the 'i's' when it comes to record keeping, tax compliance, business operations, and anything that may be of use in the future, as is the case with the other entities discussed.

You often find that this structure is used for rapidly expanding businesses, and most businesses want to expand.

Chapter Summary

Converting a business to an LLC can be done for many reasons. Before you start, check that you are able to do so in your home state or another state that you have been considering.

You may be a sole proprietor, a shareholder in a corporation, or a member of an existing LLC, and your reasons for conversion may be growth, tax breaks, or even correcting a mistake in choosing the wrong entity in the beginning, perhaps too hastily. The reasons aren't important, but the correct implementation of due process is vital.

From choosing a name, to producing articles of organization, drafting operating agreements, finding out about the role of the IRS, and business structure for optimum and effective running of your entity, nothing should be neglected.

Converting a sole proprietorship is the simplest, and although corporation conversion has more steps, such as shareholders meetings and resolutions, if you follow the steps one by one, things will go smoothly. Take into consideration liquidation and/or sale of assets, the impact on tax, and the implications thereafter, before you decide.

Making an LLC into a member of an LLC is seen as a parent company becoming part of an already existing LLC, and the same advice applies to business licenses, articles of organization, operating agreements, and all the other nitty-gritty things discussed above.

At the end of the day, do what is best for you, your LLC, or your LLC turned corporation, by following the recommendations in this chapter.

CHAPTER 6
ACCOUNTING FOR YOUR LLC

You may want to do your own bookkeeping or accounting, but you should consult a professional. It is not absolutely necessary, but a professional bookkeeper, auditor, or accountant worth their salt, will structure your LLC in the most effective way possible.

There are so many starter bookkeeping instruction manuals out there, and if your business is relatively simple, such as my former salt trading LLC, then there is no reason why you can't do your own books.

Having said that, I used an accountant as I was a bit unsure of my own ability and thought it best to use an expert. You can get started on your own but appoint a professional according to the growth of your business.

Ask yourself whether you want to pay more tax or less tax, and let your answer influence your decision in this regard. I kind of sway between doing it myself and appointing someone. When I am favoring doing it myself, I flick through my old high school accounting textbook, and it usually changes my mind, but as I have said so many times, it is a personal choice.

'General ledger' is one of the buzz phrases when it comes to accounting, auditing, and bookkeeping, so let me explain it in greater detail.

What is a General Ledger and What Does it Record?

A general ledger is used to comprehensively record all financial transactions of a business, be it a sole proprietorship, corporation, or LLC. Even if you have decided to appoint a professional, it is still important to understand the importance of a general ledger, and to get a basic idea of how it is utilized.

Let's look at some general ledger transactions.

LLC Investment Assets

These don't have to be actual tangible assets, they could be stocks, shares, NFT's, or cryptocurrency. Real estate is generally seen as a low-risk asset, and your LLC might start out small by buying an office to work from and expand its property portfolio from there.

Every amount spent in pursuit of asset investment must be recorded and backed up with the necessary sale or transfer documentation.

Equipment

Your LLC may need office equipment, let's say a large printer, which can be bought or leased. It is arguably better to lease in this situation, as breakdowns or other issues are often attended to as part of the monthly payments. Whatever the nature of the transaction, the amount must be recorded, and any relevant invoices, payment receipts, written agreements, and everything to do with that transaction or those transactions must be kept.

Income and Expenditure

This is simple, kind of. Any money that comes into your LLC and any money that leaves your LLC should be recorded in a general ledger. Credit lines to customers must match up to invoices and so must your business credit, be it from suppliers or outside credit providers.

The same applies to cash received or paid, even though actual cash in hand will become obsolete, it can't be ignored, and must be recorded in the general ledger.

At the end of the day, you don't want the IRS to discover that your accounting system is up the pole, so to speak. Also, keeping accurate records will assist tremendously if your LLC is audited. You don't want to spend days searching for receipts, invoices, statements, credit slips, and other documents that match the transactions in the general ledger.

You need to be diligent from step one.

Taxation

Any entity wants to minimize its tax obligations, and pass-through tax is a way to do so, in the case of most LLCs. Even though your LLC is the business entity, tax obligations pass through the LLC to the members. Unlike S-Corps where the corporation and its shareholders get taxed. Pass-through tax is not always the most efficient in every case, but as a general rule, most times it is.

Single-member LLC

The IRS will tax you as a sole proprietorship. Practically there is no need for pass-through tax because your LLC is just you, meaning your salary is taxed. This would be a situation where the main reason for your LLC is the protection of personal assets. Although taxed like a sole proprietorship, the LLC is not actually one.

Multiple-member LLC

In this instance, members are taxed on their personal income, equivalent to profit share, and not as a salary per se, but pass-through tax still applies.

Corporation Taxation

If your LLC is a single member, then opting to be taxed as a corporation is a simple decision based solely on percentages. There is a flat percentage tax rate of 21% for C-Corporations. If you are earning an amount that places you in the 30% plus tax bracket, then the decision is a no-brainer. Bear in mind that your LLC is still an LLC, just taxed as a corporation.

If your LLC has multiple members, then choosing to be taxed as a C-Corp may or may not save on tax. Double taxation applies because the flat rate of 21% stands, but dividends are also taxed. The decision is based on the value of dividends that you wish to pay out. It is possible that your LLC will reinvest what would be potentially paid as dividends. A possible reason for this would be a personal property rental income that pays the bills.

Payroll Taxation

If your LLC has employees, then they have to pay tax on their salaries, but your LLC also has to pay contributions. There is software that allows you to put in the salary amounts that each employee receives, and all the tax calculations are done for you. Sage Pay and QuickBooks are my favorites, from the point of view that they are simple and back-end support is available due to a monthly fee that your LLC will pay for the software usage and the service. Pricing is reasonable, and the time you save will be worth the expenditure. Below are the basic payroll taxes.

Federal Tax

Also referred to as FICA tax because it is governed by the Federal Insurance Contribution Act. Federal tax is split into two sub-categories, Social Security tax, and Medicare tax.

Social Security Tax

Part of this tax is payable by the LLC, and part is payable by the employee up to the capped amount of $160,200. The flat rate percentage is 6.2%, and the employer/employee split is 50%.

Medicare Tax

There is no earning limit on Medicare tax, and the rate is only 1.45% of earnings, also split 50/50 between employer and employee.

Local State Payroll Tax

This depends on the state in which your LLC is registered, but it covers short-term medical leave and the cost of certain basic medical care.

Unemployment Tax

Employers are responsible for these tax payments, but only on the first $7,000 of each employee's salary. In some states, if unemployment tax is paid before a certain date, then the employer is entitled to a rebate, also called a tax break. It is small things like this that you need to check out... if you don't know, you won't save.

Tax Breaks

On top of the avoidance of double taxation by taking advantage of pass-through taxes, there are tax breaks that apply to LLCs.

Qualified Business Income (QBI)

Legislation enacted in 2017 made allowance for tax breaks on QBI. The tax saving comes in on the deductible portion of self-employment tax, self-employment health insurance, and contributions to retirement plans. Your LLC can claim back 20% on the deductible portions, which is quite a significant saving.

Allowable Business Deductions

Essentially you want to make as small a profit as possible with the law. Remember that! If you work from home, you can apportion part of your rent or mortgage repayments as office rental. This is perfectly legal and should technically be equivalent to the amount of space taken up for business purposes. The best way to calculate the amount is to take the total square foot space of your house or apartment, divide your rent or mortgage by the square feet, and multiply that amount by how many square feet your work area takes up.

The same applies to internet usage, and you can split the cost of your WiFi between work-related internet use and personal internet use. Basically, you take every expense that an office is required to pay and allocate part of it to your home and the other part to your home office. Utilities, coffee, cleaning supplies, telephone costs, etc.

Donations to charities are not taxable, plus they make your business look good and make you feel good too. Paying for an employee's education also provides a tax break. If you structure your expenditure correctly, then you can save significantly on tax.

Cash versus Accrual Accounting

Accounting is essential for several reasons, and keeping your books up to date will save time in the long run. If you get into a good habit of updating your record-keeping system daily, you will set the tone for efficient long-term accounting. If you let things slide and have the attitude that you will just throw an invoice in a file and get back to it later, when later comes, you will be inundated and will probably have forgotten about aspects of a particular sale, for instance.

Tax is based on the figures that you produce, so you want accuracy, and to ensure that your books reflect the financial position of your LLC, you need to keep records of everything. Before explaining cash or accrual, I would like to give you a rundown of the basic principles of recording transactions. Some of what I will explain may sound simple or just common sense, but rather safe than sorry. I recommend using this guide when you start doing business by creating a checklist and developing a system. It won't take you long to get the hang of it, and you will no longer need the guide.

Invoices Received

Whether you are offering a service or selling a product, you will have expenses, which are paid based on invoices from service providers. For example, let's say that your LLC is a furniture manufacturer, and you are supplied with the foam that goes into cushions that come with your couches.

When you take delivery, the driver may give you an original invoice for the value of the foam delivered. Otherwise, you will receive an invoice via email. If you have the physical invoice, immediately scan it and store it in an electronic file. Then take the original and file it in a physical file. Immediately record the transaction in your accounting system, and also keep a spreadsheet. Below are examples of two possible entries:

Supplier	Product	Quantity	Del Date	Invoice Number	Due Date	Paid
XYZ Services	Foam	50 x bags	1 March 2022	001	31 March	No
ABC Services	Foam	50 x bags	1 March 2022	002	On Del	Yes

The first entry is an example of a 30-day account, where you receive an order and pay 30 days later. The second entry is an example of immediate payment.

You now possess three records documenting the transaction: a physical invoice, an electronically saved invoice, and a spreadsheet. Consider the entry into your accounting system as the fourth and final record.

Invoices Sent

These are invoices sent to customers. In this example, your customer is a hotel that has ordered furniture for their lobby. The same principle would apply, i.e., electronically stored copy of the invoice, physically filed invoice, spreadsheet, and accounting system. As a side note, your physical filing system is an individual thing. You may prefer a separate file for invoices received and invoices sent or one file with sections...up to you. The spread sheet would look something like this:

Customer	Product	Quantity	Del Date	Invoice Number	Due Date	Received
1st Hotel	Couches	5	1 March 2022	001	31 March	No
1st Hotel	Couches	5	1 March 2022	002	On Del	Yes

The above is the reverse of the invoices received spreadsheet, but the system is the same.

Proof of Other Transactions

If you take a customer or supplier for a business lunch and pay with the business credit card, then keep the bill and apply the same method as the above examples. If you write a check, you should make a copy from the duplicate and do the same thing. Even cash transactions for fungibles, such as office-cleaning materials, must be recorded.

You get the picture, but to sum it up in a sentence: keep physical, electronic, and spreadsheet records of all transactions and enter them into your accounting system immediately.

Accounting Systems

Some may argue that this accounting method is easier than accrual, and I would agree. However, I know of several LLCs that use accrual accounting. It is a personal preference, but when there are multiple daily transactions in bigger businesses, accrual makes more sense.

Cash Accounting

If your LLC is an entirely cash business, then cash accounting is the definite recommendation. When I say cash-based, I don't mean cash in hand. I mean payment on delivery by customers and payment on receipt by your LLC. There might be cash-in-hand transactions, of course, especially if you are a retailer. The method is to record cash in and cash out immediately. This system is not only reserved for cash businesses. It also works for 30-day accounts.

Accrual Accounting

Even though cash accounting can be used for 30-day account businesses, accrual is perhaps more suited to such. Accrual accounting records transactions when they happen, not when money is received or paid out. To go back to the foam delivery example on a 30-day account basis. Receipt of the foam is the transaction, so it is recorded on the day the foam is received, meaning that the entry is taken care of already by the time the money changes hands.

Did You Notice the Contradictions?

I said that immediate records must be kept, so you may be thinking that cash and accrual accounting is then the same thing. Not quite. The spread sheet will look similar for both, but the actual entries in your books will differ—cash when the money is received and accrual when the transaction occurs.

The General Ledger

This accounting document, which is relatively simple, could be said to be the basis of accounting and is used to record the following:

- Assets: Company cars, equipment, and office furniture.

- Liabilities: Loans owed to banks, unpaid rent, or money owed to suppliers.

- Income: Money generated from sales or service provision.

- Expenses: Telephone account, suppliers paid, or operating expenses.

- Equity: Assets less liabilities

It may seem difficult to understand if you don't have accounting trading. Below are a few very simple examples to show the principle. In order to learn more, you can find three-day accounting courses that teach you the basics. Even if you have an outside person doing your books, a course is still a good idea. A general ledger needs to balance, i.e., the left column and right column need to add up to the same amount.

Example 1:

Description	Debit	Credit
Cash in account	50,000	
Owner investment		50,000
TOTAL	50,000	50,000

Usually, there would be a date of the transaction, but I want to give only the crucial information. The above transaction shows that the owner invested $50,000, and the investment is sitting in the LLCs bank account. The above is what a general ledger would look like on the day of the birth of your business.

Example 2:

Description	Debit	Credit
Cash in account	30,000	
Owner investment		50,000
Appliances purchased	20,000	
TOTAL	50,000	50,000

In this example, the LLC is an appliance sales business. The member investment is the same, but the LLC has used $20,000 of the cash to buy appliances.

Example 3:

Description	Debit	Credit
Cash in account	30,000	
Owner investment		50,000
Appliances purchased for cash	15,000	

Appliances purchased on credit	15,000	
TOTAL	50,000	50,000

In this one, the member investment is also the same, but half of the appliances have been purchased for cash, and the other half on credit. The cash is thus gone, but the credit amount will only become due at the end of the month. It still has to be recorded in order to balance the books, even though it has not left the account.

The principle is simple, but if you are paying out 20 invoices a day and receiving 15 payments a day, it gets complicated, not in terms of that principle, but in terms of the time and concentration required.

How to Set Up Your Bookkeeping System

Whether you have decided on accrual basis accounting or cash basis accounting, you will have to set up a bookkeeping system, of which there are several. I will take you through the three most relevant and commonly used systems to allow you to make an informed decision.

Do It Yourself Bookkeeping

This is more suited to small businesses, and you can simply use an excel spreadsheet to track income and expenses. You also have the option of using a cloud-based system of bookkeeping, which are very reasonably priced. My personal recommendations would be SagePay or

QuickBooks, as they are very user friendly, and back system support is very good.

You have to be very disciplined in this case, you can't leave the books for weeks and tell yourself that you will attend to them at a later stage. When you reach that later stage, you will have created so much extra work for yourself, and the possibility of big confusion.

Outsourced Bookkeeping

You don't want to appoint a huge accounting firm that charges an arm and a leg, so an actual bookkeeper would be fine. There are quite a few bookkeepers that do freelance work after they retire, so ask around and get referrals before choosing someone for the position.

Also, you need to check their work, and even though your bookkeeper should be an expert, mistakes can happen. I have found, through experience, that I have better relationships with bookkeepers, well more accountants, when they send me work to run my eyes over and approve, alternatively raise concerns.

In-House Bookkeeping

This will become necessary if you are spending too much time on the bookkeeping side yourself, instead of focusing on making money, or if your outsourced bookkeeper becomes out of their depth. It will be the costliest method but will probably be justified in these circumstances.

Make sure you get the right person, just in the earlier case of the right manager.

How to Keep Track of Your Expenses

Your expenses are obviously recorded no matter what bookkeeping system you choose, and please remember that every entry into your books needs to be backed by the necessary documentation.

If you have a business meeting over lunch, you need to keep a copy of the receipt. The same applies to company credit card purchases, such as flights to attend a conference. Monthly accounts from service providers, such as your electricity and water bill or office phone statement, must also be kept. You get the idea.

Develop a good filing system and make sure you are aware of the legislation in the state(s) where your business is registered. By law, you have to keep certain records for X number of years, usually between three and ten years, but it is not a bad idea to hang onto your records indefinitely.

There are companies that provide file storage facilities, but they come with a cost, and the risk of your business information being accessible to others is high (hypothetically).

Chapter Summary

Accounting is especially important for tax purposes, record keeping, and forecasting. You can, of course, do it yourself, but may prefer to use an expert. Essentially you need to keep and maintain a general ledger, to record investment or equipment purchases, income and expenses, and any miscellaneous transactions that impact your business.

You need to decide on your tax system, and complete the correct IRS forms, whether you want to be taxed as a partnership, sole proprietorship, or corporation.

Next, you need to assess whether you use the accrual or cash system of bookkeeping. Accrual usually works best with accounts, and I gave the 30-day example. Income and expenditure is recorded before it leaves or arrives in your account, whereas the cash system details cash out when it leaves, and cash in when it arrives.

You may want to keep your books yourself, on a spreadsheet, or using cloud-based software, otherwise outsource or hire an in-house bookkeeper. When making the decision, consider that your primary role should be making the business successful.

Keeping records of expenses is important, and backup documents, such as receipts or credit card statements, must be filed and kept for a certain period, depending on which state(s) your LLC is registered in.

All of this is very important, and if done correctly, will save you heaps of time if you are audited by the IRS, or are required to produce records for any other reason.

CHAPTER 7
FILING TAXES AS AN LLC

T ax season—nobody's favorite—is very necessary. Well, maybe a favorite of the accountants and bookkeepers. There is a huge honesty element here, and I would strongly advise you not to hide anything from the IRS, not even once. You need to be able to sleep at night, knowing that you are compliant.

Consider that taxation depends on the number of members of your LLC. As I have stated previously, your LLC can be taxed as a corporation, which may save you money when it comes to IRS payments. LLCs can certainly have non-taxable deductions, but it is vital that you hit the filing deadlines to avoid penalties.

So, here is some information on what needs to be done to be compliant. Don't forget that there are different challenges in terms of different business structures, but they should be expected and anticipated.

Requirements for Single Member LLCs

A sole proprietorship and a single member LLC are treated in exactly the same way by the IRS. They are basically identical, except, obviously, the LLC provides that personal protection. Either way, the IRS requires that you file a personal tax return. See the links in the previous chapter, where you can get the necessary forms, from the IRS website. There is an extra step for a single member LLC, and that is filing the Schedule C, profit or loss report for the business.

Pretty straightforward; revenue, less business expenditure, equals profit or loss (hopefully profit). Revenue is simpler, being whatever money comes in, whether you sell a product or sell your time. Expenditure is anything from office rental, telephone costs, fuel for business related travel, purchasing products, to wages for temps, or printer repairs. Basically, any necessary costs of running your business. The end figure of this calculation is added to your personal tax filings.

Requirements for Multiple Member LLCs

Whether your LLC has two or ten members, or any amount from two upwards, it is seen as a partnership by the IRS. To put it in simple terms, members are taxed on their personal profits, which will usually correspond with the amount invested by said members.

On the form 1065, being the US Return of Partnership Income, the LLC is required to submit its profit and loss statement, along with a declaration of deductible expenses. Next, your balance sheet shows all financial information from beginning to end of the tax year, and this is where accurate record keeping is vital.

Another form, just a one-pager, is needed; Schedule K-1, part of the 1065. This lays out the different percentage shares of the members, which allows the IRS to examine personal profits.

Schedule E records the profits and losses of each individual member of the LCC.

All the forms should be filed together to show that tax is being taken seriously, but also because it provides for less administration. You always want to be seen as timeous and See the forms on the IRS website.

Chapter Summary

Taxation depends on a few factors. Single member LLCs are taxed on the difference between revenue and expenses, as is a sole proprietorship.

Multiple member LLCs require a profit and loss statement and an itemized set of deductible expenses in order to comply with IRS regulations.

You have the choice of a C-Corp or an S-corp. For the former, there has to be a board of directors, appointed shareholders, formal issuing of shares, and defining of business positions. In these instances, the LLC files and the members also file in their personal capacity. S-corps have different requirements, such as domestic domicile, and a 100-member limit on shareholders, amongst others.

Using fixed and variable income and expenses, you can produce an estimate of your taxes. Social Security and Medicare taxes must be considered and depending on turnover factors and specific non-taxable medical expenses, you will be able to arrive at figures, as to your tax benefits.

If you follow the above, with help from professionals if needed, you can rest easy that the IRS is happy.

Just a quick bit of advice. I often skip ahead when reading a document, assuming that I have full knowledge, and I am most often incorrect. Don't do that! Follow the links that pertain to your business situation and read *and* understand the requirements as thoroughly as possible.

CHAPTER 8
DISSOLVING AN LLC

There are several reasons for dissolving an LLC, and this is where limiting your liability comes into play. Not in every case, but you should have peace of mind, that you are protected in a situation where dissolution is forced due to circumstance.

When Should You Dissolve Your LLC?

The short answer is that you should dissolve your LLC when the purpose of that LLC has been completed or if continuing to operate your LLC is no longer financially viable. These are the reasons why you created an LLC in the first place.

If the Purpose for Creating the LLC Has Been Fulfilled/ Come to an End

This is pretty straightforward, your LLC may have been formed with an expiration date, generally depending on the occurrence of a likely future event. This doesn't mean that the business has to stop operating when that point is reached. You may have a specific plan and want to restructure, for instance.

The purpose of the LLC may be to tender for a supply contract, that is a once off, for say 12 months. When the contract has come to an end, and your LLC has been compliant in every regard, especially tax, you can then dissolve it. This will be recorded in the beginning, of course.

If Financial Viability No Longer Exists

If your LLC is continually making losses and you have taken every measure that you can in order to mitigate the situation but with no success, then you are compelled to dissolve the LLC.

Some measures could be making employees redundant, which is always terrible, and something that should only be done in extreme circumstances. Otherwise, you can look at payment arrangements with overdue creditors or extension of payment deadlines. An investor may help, but if your LLC is really struggling, the likelihood of that is limited.

Unfortunately, many businesses face closure, and often through outside influences; the most obvious example being Covid-19. You don't ever want your LLC to be in such a position, but at least you have that personal protection.

Types of Dissolution

I mentioned financial viability, and if you are for all intents and purposes a broke LLC, you are said to be bankrupt. You can voluntarily dissolve your LLC, but you may encounter dissolution at the hands of creditors, which is then classified as involuntary.

Let's say your LLC has credit with a bank, and it also owes your supplier a large sum of money. Either one of these creditors can apply to have your LLC dissolved, in the hope that they will get at least some of what they are owed through the sale of LLC assets and seizure of cash.

Voluntary Dissolution

This does not only apply to lack of financial viability, but it does apply in cases where the purpose of the LLC has come to an end. Let's have a look at the steps to follow.

Consider a scenario where a group of friends united to start a weekend hiking gear rental LLC called "Adventure Essentials." Over time, the members found joy in providing gear for local hiking enthusiasts. However, as life takes its course, they realize that their initial purpose, centered around weekend adventures, has naturally concluded.

In this context, voluntary dissolution becomes a consideration not due to financial struggles but rather as a mindful choice aligning with the fulfilled purpose. The friends decide to formally close "Adventure Essentials" and begin a new chapter.

The steps to follow involve unanimous agreement among members to dissolve the LLC, settling any outstanding debts, notifying creditors and government agencies, and distributing any remaining assets among themselves. Through this voluntary dissolution, the members gracefully close the door on "Adventure Essentials," cherishing the memories and lessons learned during their shared journey.

You Have to Vote to Dissolve the LLC

Your operating agreement should provide details as to dissolution, but if it doesn't, then the members will have to vote to decide if the purpose for creating the LLC has ended. It may be the death of a shareholder, or as I mentioned previously, the end of a once off contract.

These events are referred to as dissolution triggers, and whether specified or not, and whether a vote is required or not, the decision to dissolve the LLC must be recorded and filed with the LLC's records.

Financial viability may require a vote, but if the situation is so dire, all members should easily agree to dissolve the LLC for personal protection.

Imagine you and your friends co-founded an LLC, "Creative Harmony Studios," to collaborate on artistic projects. Your operating agreement serves as the guiding script for the LLC's journey. However, unforeseen events unfold – perhaps the unexpected passing of a key member or the completion of a major, one-time project.

In the absence of specific dissolution details in the operating agreement, the LLC members gather for a crucial vote. They discuss the triggering events, referred to as dissolution triggers, and collectively decide whether the LLC's purpose has reached its natural conclusion.

The decision-making process involves considering various factors, such as the loss of a key contributor or the successful completion of a unique project. Even if financial viability is at stake, a unanimous vote may lean towards dissolution for the collective well-being of all members.

Once the decision is reached, whether by vote or consensus, it's imperative to record and file the dissolution decision with the LLC's records. This ensures that the journey of "Creative Harmony Studios" is properly documented, providing closure to this chapter of collaborative creativity.

Filing Your Final Tax Return

If you still owe the IRS money, or are not up to date with your returns, then you will have to prepare and submit your final return, and pay whatever tax is required or claim tax refunds payable to your LLC.

Once this process is completed, your LLC will be compliant and will be issued with some form of compliance certificate or letter of compliance, which differ from state to state. You do have to indicate on your return that it is your final one, and that the reason is dissolution of your LLC.

Obviously, you have to file the returns associated with your choice of taxation, and that may include federal tax returns, as well as employment tax returns, without which you will not be compliant.

Filing an Article of Dissolution

This is an official request for the state to allow dissolution of your LLC. A standard form to assist you can be found on the Secretary of State website.

The form requires business information, as well as details of the members and recordable asset distribution. Perhaps you had to sell assets to settle debts. Your liabilities must also be specified. Look at it as a short story of your LLC's position at the time, how you arrived at that position, followed by a request for your certificate of dissolution.

You will have to pay a small fee and file the certificate with your business records. You should remember me saying earlier that records have to be kept for certain amounts of time. This applies even in cases of dissolution.

Settling Outstanding Debts

This may be difficult, especially if you are in a financial situation where further business operations are not viable.

Even if not specifically required, you should notify your creditors that you would like to settle their accounts, and request that they put in claims for you to ascertain final figures.

The same applies if you can only partly pay or cannot pay at all. You will have to notify them of your inability to pay and request that they put in claims against your LLC.

Procedures differ depending on your state, and you may have to publish a notice calling on your creditors to submit claims, or pin notices up at the court which has jurisdiction.

The general idea is to use all money and assets owned by the business to pay, or at least partially pay, creditors.

Sale or Distribution of Assets

If you are fortunate enough to have assets remaining after settling all your LLC's debt, those assets will be sold and the proceeds distributed amongst the members, alternatively the physical assets are distributed.

The distribution process, and what may be distributed can be obtained from your operating agreement, or according to state law.

Complete Other Winding Down Processes

You will have to notify customers, suppliers, service providers, and employees of the dissolution. This should all be in writing, or you can call meetings with the above entities or people, then follow up with written confirmation.

Closing Bank Accounts

The last task is to close your business bank account(s) and "retire" both your federal and state taxation identification number.

And just like that, your LLC has been dissolved, and any liability of that LLC, does not pass on to you, and/or other members.

Involuntary Dissolution

This may be the result if your LLC becomes bankrupt, if shareholders cannot agree on dissolution, if there is evidence of fraud, or if the LLC does not comply with tax and legal requirements.

The court will enforce dissolution in cases like this, but more specifically, creditors will kick off dissolution procedures in the hope that the LLC has enough money and assets to settle their claims.

Once the creditors are settled, or partially settled from actual money and money raised by sale of assets, the members are exempt from personal liability relating to outstanding amounts owed to creditors.

The same process of notifying customers, creditors, suppliers, etc., applies, although the court is more involved, meaning that notices are kind of done for your LLC.

Just like voluntary dissolution, tax has to be up to date, and the process ends with a certificate of dissolution, or a letter to the same effect, after the state is satisfied that your LLC has complied with all requirements.

From that point, no member is liable in any capacity for outstanding business debts, but do not forget about…

The Exception, Personal Surety

Avoid signing personal surety because that negates the whole point of limited liability. If you do sign personal surety, and the LLC owes the bank a substantial amount, you, as the surety, become liable as a natural person.

Unfortunately, some banks and financiers will not give credit to an LLC if nobody is prepared to stand personal surety, but 'private' investors may not enforce the same requirement.

Personal suretyship can be seen as a convention to limit the liability of credit providers, so try your best not to be put in a position where a deal won't go through without some form of surety.

Chapter Summary

When an LLC has completed the purpose for which it was created, you can voluntarily dissolve the LLC by sole decision if you are the only member, or via a vote if you are part of a multiple member LLC.

You will have to file your final tax return, as well as your articles of dissolution (the story of the business, and why its purpose has been completed).

The LLC's debts must be settled, and this may involve selling assets. It may be the case that the sale of assets and liquid cash in the business bank account don't raise enough to pay off all creditors, in which case, when dissolution is complete, those creditors cannot come after your personal assets.

In an involuntary dissolution, your creditors may apply for dissolution, but thereafter the process is the same and your personal assets are still protected.

You also need to wind everything down by informing your customers and employees through due process.

Finally, you will need to terminate contracts with service providers and close the business bank account(s).

A word of warning, *never* sign as a personal surety because it negates the limitation of your liability.

CHAPTER 9
GOVERNMENT CONTRACTS

Any form of ongoing contract is a great financial opportunity for any business, and they are a lot easier to obtain than one may think. Having said that, there is a protocol that must be followed, and if done correctly could result in a decent amount of ongoing work.

Interestingly, the United States government is sometimes referred to as the 'largest customer in the world,' because in terms of national and international purchasing of anything from tractors to watches to fruit, the spend is more than any other country. Based on this, the law requires the U.S. government to allow small businesses opportunities for growth, through awarding of ongoing contracts. The further reasons cited are as follows:

- To ensure that large businesses don't "muscle out" small businesses

- To gain access to the new ideas that small businesses provide

- To support small businesses as engines of economic development and job creation

- To offer opportunities to disadvantaged socio-economic groups

Below is a detailed guide as to what your LLC needs to do in order to be considered for a government contract. You can do the process on your own, but prepare for delays, as the civil service is inundated generally, so backlogs do occur.

My recommendation is not to rush, but rather to set yourself small goals and work through the admin step by step.

Step 1 - Obtain a Unique Entity Identifier

Referred to by the acronym UEI, this is like a social security number for a business. The easiest way to do this is to go to Sam.gov, then click on 'Register Entity' and follow the prompts from there. You will have to enter all the details of your LCC, such as address, registered office, member details, and so on. All the information will be on the documentation that you received after registering your LLC.

Step 2 - Obtain a NAICS code

When you have your UIE number then you will need to get a North American Industry Classification System code. The code

is linked to the nature of your business. For example a furniture wholesalers code will be SIC 571 and a food producer will be: NAICS 311. The code is so that the Census Bureau can keep accurate statistics and so that your business is easily identifiable.

Go to NAICS.com and browse the categories to find the code that your LLCs industry falls into.

Step 3 - Register your business with SAM

Go back to the SAM site and enter the required details, i.e., size of entity, location, turnover, capabilities etc. This allows the Federal government contractors to find your business based on a search as to what type of work they require. For instance, if a food supply contract is on offer, a search will bring up all the businesses in that sphere, allowing the government to make contact in pursuance of a possible supply contract.

Step 4 - Comply with Public Labor Laws

Your LLC should be compliant from the outset, but to check if the correct employment contracts are in place, and that your employees are getting the correct benefits, will ensure that you do not miss government contract opportunities. Outsource this to a labour lawyer. The money spent will be worth making certain that everything is in order by a specialist in the field.

Picture this: you've launched "GreenScape Eco Solutions," an LLC focused on sustainable landscaping services. Recognizing the significance of environmental compliance and ethical labor practices, you diligently approach Step 4 – Comply with Public Labor Laws.

Acknowledging the intricacies of employment contracts in the landscaping industry and the importance of fair treatment for your employees, you opt to enlist the expertise of a labor lawyer. This legal professional meticulously reviews your employment contracts, ensuring they align with labor laws, and verifies that your employees receive the rightful benefits.

Consider this step as planting the seeds for ethical and compliant business growth. Just as a conscientious gardener tends to each plant's specific needs to ensure a thriving garden, securing the guidance of a labor lawyer nurtures a work environment where rules are followed, benefits are just, and your LLC stands tall in its commitment to both employees and regulatory standards. Through an investment, the assurance of compliance and ethical labor practices becomes an integral part of the flourishing landscape that is "GreenScape Eco Solutions."

Step 5 - Make Sure that Your Cybersecurity System is up to Date

Like Step 4, this should be taken care of from the outset of LLC registration, or preferably when you buy your electronic devices. This is beneficial to your LLC anyway, because you want to keep your data secure, no matter what industry you are in.

For example, you've established an LLC, "TechGuard Innovations," specializing in cutting-edge software solutions. From the moment of LLC registration and the procurement of electronic devices, you prioritize cybersecurity as a fundamental aspect of your business strategy.

Upon setting up your IT infrastructure, you implement robust cybersecurity measures, including firewalls, encryption, and regular software updates. This ensures that your innovative software projects, client data, and internal information remain secure from potential cyber threats.

Consider this approach as building a fortress around your digital kingdom. Just as you'd fortify the walls of a castle to protect its treasures, fortifying your cybersecurity defenses becomes an ongoing commitment. By incorporating cybersecurity from the outset, "TechGuard Innovations" establishes a culture of data protection, fostering trust among clients and stakeholders in the rapidly evolving landscape of technology solutions.

CHAPTER 10
S-CORPORATIONS EXPLAINED

To comprehend S-Corps more effectively, it's essential to first establish a general understanding of what constitutes a corporation. Shareholders, also known as stockholders, possess ownership stakes in a corporation, with the extent of ownership determined by the percentage of stock or shares held. In essence, the ownership structure varies based on the quantity of shares acquired.

It's crucial to recognize the legal distinction between a corporation and its owners. From a legal standpoint, a corporation is regarded as a distinct entity or "person." For instance, if a corporation has two shareholders, the total count is three individuals: the two natural persons who are shareholders and the corporation itself, acknowledged as a juristic person.

Of course, a corporation is not a living and breathing entity, but it is a separate "person" in terms of the law. Arguably the biggest advantage of being a shareholder in a corporation is that if the corporation goes bankrupt, the person does not. Many decisions as to corporations are based on the legal protection afforded to their shareholders.

A corporation can have a solitary shareholder, meaning that 100% of that corporation is owned by one person. Additionally, a corporation can have as many as 100 shareholders, which means that 100 people each have a percentage share in the corporation. Don't forget that each one of those shareholders has independent rights, as does the corporation.

There are crossovers between corporations, and there are six generally recognized types of corporations, but for these purposes, you need to be aware of three of them. I will cover Limited Liability Companies (LLCs), C-Corporations (C-Corps), and Non-Profit Corporations briefly before moving on to S-Corps in great detail. It is important to understand the basics of LLCs, and C-Corps.

Limited Liability Companies (LLCs)

An LLC, or Limited Liability Company, is a business structure that combines aspects of a corporation and a partnership or sole proprietorship. It provides its owners, known as members, with limited liability for the company's debts and obligations. This means that the personal assets of the members are generally protected from the company's creditors, and their liability is typically limited to the amount they have invested in the business.

An LLC can have multiple members or be owned singularly (single-member LLC). LLCs do not require a board of directors and are very flexible in terms of operating requirements and tax filings, meaning that there is a lot less paperwork. Other than that, the attraction is the actual limitation of personal liability, meaning that any personal assets owned in the private name of the LLC owner or owners are safe from repossession in any litigation situation.

However, a minor complication may arise if the LLC has multiple owners, and one of them either passes away or resigns from the business. In such cases, the LLC could be dissolved and subsequently re-formed, potentially under a different name, depending on the intentions of the remaining owner or owners.

C-Corporation

A C corporation, often referred to as a C corp (designated for its position in subchapter "C" of the Internal Revenue Code), functions as a separate legal entity with ownership held by its shareholders. A board of directors is required, and the C-Corp is run by the board of directors and the shareholders. C-Corps are subject to double taxation and cannot pass through shareholder profits. This means that the C-Corp is taxed on profits as a corporation, and its shareholders are taxed on the remaining profits as distributed amongst said shareholders. Larger businesses are best served as C-Corps, as it is the appropriate business structure when targeting growth.

Major American companies such as Microsoft and Walmart operate as C corporations, meaning their income is subject to taxation under Subchapter C of the US Internal Revenue Code.

If you have the intention of working towards offering stock and becoming a public corporation, a C-Corp is the right vehicle for your business. C-Corps also offer the protection of limiting liability, thus ensuring that personal assets are completely separate from assets owned by the C-Corp.

Non-profit Businesses

These types of businesses are not relevant to corporations discussed in this book, but as the name suggests, non-profits just look to cover costs and are most often public-service-orientated, like museums, schools, or hospitals. Charities also fall under this business type, and their taxation rules are largely reduced.

Do NOT set up a non-profit business that is actually for profit in order to dodge tax. It is illegal and will have an effect on your future ability to hold corporate positions.

S-Corporations

An S corporation stands as a unique form of corporation deliberately crafted to address the issue of double taxation inherent in conventional corporate structures. Consequently, millions of S corporations exist across the United States, including entities such as retail stores, banks, car dealerships, and movie theaters.

Before an S-Corp is born, your business must be set up as a corporation by filing what is called "Articles of Incorporation." The aforesaid is a set of legal documentation informing the Secretary of State of the details relevant to your business, such as name, address, and type. Once the corporation is registered, shareholders must sign and submit Form 2553 to make the corporation an S-Corp. From this juncture onwards, taxes are handled individually by each shareholder. The IRS imposes the following requirements to be met in order to attain S-Corporation status:

- be domiciled in the USA

- have 100 shareholders or less

- have only allowable shareholders

- have only one class of stock

- not be ineligible on any grounds

Be Domiciled in the USA

The simple explanation is that if you don't live in the United States, you cannot be a shareholder. There are a few arbitrary exceptions, such as spending time out of the country working or having a second fixed address in another country. This isn't something to worry about, an expert can provide advice if you do find yourself in a situation similar to the one above.

Have 100 Shareholders or Less

This is self-explanatory but do remember that C-Corps can have over 100 shareholders, so no further information is needed.

Have Only Allowable Shareholders

Certain people and entities are precluded from being shareholders in S-Corps, namely, non-residents, foreign trusts, individual retirement accounts, multiple member LLCs, limited liability partnerships, and C-corps.

Have Only One Class of Stock

Because S-Corps can only have one class of stock, they can only have one class of investors, which can be limiting, as dividends and distribution rights cannot vary outside the equivalence of shareholding. Depending on size, having a 100-shareholder limit may be a disadvantage, and one has to remember that foreign ownership, as well as shareholding by other business vehicles such as trusts, is prohibited.

Not Be Ineligible on Any Grounds

This applies to individuals who are still minors, people with criminal records, or any other ineligibility that may arise outside of these categories, such as being under investigation for fraud or having previously declared bankruptcy.

Advantages of S-Corps

Protected Assets

All shareholders are exempt from personal liability for any business liabilities or business debt. That mea[ns that as a shareholder, your house, car, or any other assets cannot be repossessed in pursuance of money owed by the S-Corp. This exemption can be waived if a shareholder signs as surety on a loan for the business, which is very inadvisable.

Asset protection is linked to the S-Corp being its own person, separate from its shareholders, which is not the case for sole proprietorships and general partnerships. Bearing in mind that your personal liability is protected, it would not be a good idea to register personal assets in your S-Corp. For instance, if you register a motor vehicle in the name of the S-Corp, you open yourself up to having that motor vehicle repossessed to cover your business debt if a judgment is obtained against the S-Corp or if bankruptcy is declared.

Pass-through Taxation

Federal taxes do not apply to S-Corps, meaning that any taxation is passed through to the shareholders, who file returns with the IRS in their personal capacity. This is especially useful as losses can offset other personal income, which means less tax. Due to shareholders receiving salaries, the tax is referred to as payroll tax.

Tax-Favorable Characterization of Income

This is basically assigning income to a category. For instance, income may be drawn as a salary by shareholders, or alternatively, dividends can be distributed to the extent that they are tax-free. Running taxation this way allows the reduction of self-employment tax while still generating business expenses and wages paid as deductions for the S-Corp. (CT Corporation Staff, 2022).

Straightforward Transfer of Ownership

Transfer of ownership or shareholding is simple, does not involve property-based adjustments, and does not attract adverse tax consequences. There is no transfer tax or capital gains tax, nor are there any tax penalties (CT Corporation Staff, 2022). This is something that can easily be done by owners or shareholders without professional assistance.

Cash Method of Accounting

Unless an S-Corp has inventory, cash accounting may be used. It is more simple than accrual accounting. The former is a method where receipts are recorded when they are actually received, and expenses are recorded when they are paid. Accrual accounting recognizes an invoice as soon as it is produced, whether it is your company invoicing for services or your company being invoiced. There may come a point where accrual accounting, although more complicated, will be a time saver.

You do get hybrid accounting, which is a mixture of cash and accrual-based accounting, but that will be covered in greater detail later in this book.

Greater Credibility

A sole proprietorship or partnership may give the impression of a small owner-operated business, but an S-Corp evidence professionalism and commitment to the business. Identifying credibility with potential customers, suppliers, and even potential employees is a good way to grow a business effectively. Having said that, it is not a good idea to puff your business up, and you probably shouldn't fake it until you make it, as the saying goes. Honesty and integrity must be maintained.

Disadvantages of S-Corps

Formation and Ongoing Expenses

As mentioned above, you are required to file Articles of Incorporation, which means obtaining a registering agent and paying the associated fee for that person's services. Some states actually impose franchise tax fees and other ongoing fees, such as annual reporting fees. The fees are not outrageous but bear in mind that these fees are not payable by sole proprietors or general partnerships.

Tax Qualification Obligations

Mistakes in terms of filing requirements can cause accidental termination of S-Corp status. This will mean that your S-Corp is taxed as a tax-paying entity under Subchapter C, as above. It doesn't happen often, and it can be corrected, but it is something to be aware of.

The Calendar Year

An S-Corp tax year must be a calendar year; this is not a major disadvantage, but it can be an admin headache. Appointing a tax expert is a good idea. Such a person does not need to be a full-time employee; however, if your business gets to the point where your taxes become complicated, it may be a good idea to hire someone full-time.

Stock Ownership Restrictions

Because S-Corps can only have one class of stock, it can only have one class of investors, which can be limiting, as dividends and distribution rights cannot vary outside the equivalence to shareholding. Depending on size, having a 100-shareholder limit may be a disadvantage, and one has to remember that foreign ownership, as well as shareholding by other business vehicles such as trusts, is prohibited.

Closer IRS Scrutiny

The IRS pays closer attention to S-Corps, largely because of wages being recharacterized as dividends. The reason for this is that if there is a recharacterization, the S-Corp will be subject to a compensatory deduction. Recharacterization may also work the other way, where dividends are considered wages. This situation makes the S-Corp liable for the employment tax liability.

Less Flexibility in Allocating Income and Loss

Income and/or losses cannot be allocated to shareholders specifically. That is because of one class of stock restrictions (Pierce, M). Stock ownership results in income and loss areas as per percentage shareholding, which is different from partnerships and LLCs, where allocation can be done via the partnership or operating agreement.

Taxable Fringe Benefits in S-Corps

S-Corp shareholders that hold a share portfolio over 2%, are taxed on fringe benefits. Considering that 2% is a very small percentage amount, it is relative to the total number of shareholders. This means that the 2% limit is a proportionate measure, considering the overall ownership distribution among shareholders. The taxation of fringe benefits is applicable to those shareholders who surpass this ownership threshold, highlighting the nuanced approach taken by the Internal Revenue Service (IRS) in regulating the tax treatment of S-Corporation shareholders based on their level of ownership.

S-Corp vs. LLC: Selecting the Right Business Structure

S-Corps and LLCs are most closely related to the six generally accepted entities, and the choice between the two may be a difficult one. They both have advantages and disadvantages, and for the purposes of thoroughness, it is important to identify those as well as any overlaps that might sway you from one to the other.

Firstly, the limitation of liability; both types of entities enjoy limited liability, meaning that only assets registered in the name of the entity can be used in bankruptcy to pay any debts or part thereof. It is advisable to limit company assets, and if you are involved in the type of work that doesn't require many assets, then all the better. No person or company wants to go bankrupt; however, shareholders or members of either entity have the peace of mind that if anything does go wrong financially, personal assets are safe from creditors.

Both S-Corps and LLCs have their tax advantages, and taxation on personal income is one of those mutual advantages. LLCs are better suited for sole proprietorships and partnerships, while S-Corps are better suited for businesses with multiple shareholders. That is not to say that a sole proprietor cannot register an S-Corp.

A pro that S-Corps enjoy over LLCs is oversight, which lends itself to greater liability. Because LLCs are a business type, an LLC can also be an S-Corp, the reason being that an S-Corp is a tax classification and not actually a type of business.

Pros and Cons of an S-Corp

Pros

S-Corps do not pay federal taxes, which is a big money-saving opportunity. The professionalism of an S-Corp can go far to establish a good reputation and grow faster than perhaps a sole proprietorship, for example. Employees can receive dividends, which provides for the ability to incentivize and should motivate quality employees, which can only enhance a business.

Cons

There are four states that tax S-Corps as actual corporations: Michigan, California, New Jersey, and New York. So, this would only be a con if you were a resident of such a state. Columbia, New Hampshire, and Tennessee do not recognize S-Corps at all, so like the four states already mentioned, it is only a con if you live in one of the three that do not recognize S-Corps. S-Corps also have a lot of regulations and guidelines to be followed, and as a result of the oversight, the owners and shareholders have less control.

Chapter Summary

Stockholders, otherwise referred to as shareholders are the owners of an S-Corp. Percentage ownership is directly proportional to percentage shareholding. If there are 100 shares and you own 20 shares, that means that you are regarded as a 20% owner. Any confusion or potential disagreements are prevented by this largely practical regulation.

An S-Corp is its own separate person, which means that owners are separate from their S-Corp. Such members cannot exceed 100, and in an S-Corp with, say, 60 shareholders, each shareholder is independent in the same way that a single shareholder is independent. Shareholders enjoy limited liability, meaning that personal assets are exempt from anything having to do with the business. Bankruptcy is the best example, and if it does happen, then shareholders have peace of mind knowing that their assets are safe.

Articles of Incorporation are the set of documentation that must be filed with the Secretary of State, informing the department of the details of your S-Corp. If you are not domiciled in America, you are precluded from being a shareholder. Only one class of stock is permitted, shareholding cannot exceed 100, and potential shareholders must be allowable as shareholders.

The major advantages of an S-Corp are personal asset protection, as well as pass-through taxation. Because federal taxes are inapplicable, losses can offset alternative personal income, which means less tax. If one needs to appoint a new shareholder or if a shareholder wants to sell his or her shares to another person, then the ownership transfer is very simple.

S-Corps are permitted to use cash accounting. That is the recording of transactions as they happen. This is a straightforward method, as opposed to accrual-based accounting, which treats income and expenditure as immediate when an invoice is raised. That means that your books will reflect money that is not yet in your account, so it can become confusing.

Greater credibility is associated with S-Corps due to the business commitment shown and the oversight required.

Expenses are a reality, and when filing Articles of Incorporation, there are fees, which may include agent fees or annual reporting fees. Tax qualification obligations must be understood carefully, and even though they are not complicated, a lack of knowledge could cause errors. The ramifications are the accidental termination of the S-Corp, which thus becomes a tax-paying entity instead of passing through tax to members.

S-Corps have to run the tax year as a calendar year, and it is advisable to get an expert to set that part up. Stock ownership is restricted due to the shareholding being directly proportional to the dividends and distribution rights. Foreign ownership is prohibited, and entities such as trusts cannot be shareholders.

S-Corps are closely scrutinized by the IRS, and there is less flexibility in the allocation of income and loss, compared to a sole proprietorship, as a comparison. Fringe benefits are taxed, and one only has to hold over 2% of shares to be subject to tax on fringe benefits.

S-Corps don't enjoy major advantages over LLCs, but the latter is more suited to sole proprietors and small partnerships. Unfortunately, there are four states in which S-Corps are taxed as corporations and a further three states that don't recognize S-Corps at all.

At this point, you should have a good overview of S-Corps and the information related to them, so I will now turn to their suitability for different types of businesses.

CHAPTER 11
HOW TO KNOW IF AN S-CORPORATION IS RIGHT FOR YOUR BUSINESS

B usinesses are all different; some people sell their time, such as lawyers, accountants, or therapists. Others sell their skills; plumbers or electricians come to mind. In addition, people sell things or provide services, and each of these profit-generating vocations requires the correct business vehicle to best serve the needs of the specific business.

The other big consideration is money; depending on turnover, salaries, expenses, and assets, an S-Corp may or may not be best for your business. Before I turn to look more practically at the money side, it is necessary to briefly touch on the two simplest business types.

The Sole Proprietorship

The name indicates that this type of business vehicle involves only one person, which is correct, but that is not to say that you cannot have other people in the business, i.e., employees. As a sole proprietor, you can have employees, but in terms of tax, the IRS sees you and your sole proprietorship as one and the same. This means that there are no forms to be filled out or registrations to be made; it is just a case of getting on with it.

The business owner must file profits or losses with his or her federal tax returns. The self-employment tax payable includes Social Security and Medicare taxes. There are dangers to a sole proprietorship, but the reason that so many of them exist is because of the zero set-up costs. If you don't have financial resources when starting a brand new business, then setting up an entity with limited liability will be impossible. This means greater risk, but the flip side is that you have complete control, formation is quick, and preparing your tax filings is easy.

The major disadvantage of a sole proprietorship is that if your business goes bankrupt then so do you. Any assets that you own, whether used specifically in the auspices of the business, or otherwise, are at risk. In a bankruptcy scenario, your creditors can repossess anything. If you have a cleaning business and you have bought several sets of industrial cleaning equipment, ownership is seen as no different from ownership of a house or car, or furniture that is not used in the operation of your business. I would argue that the non-existence of liability limitation is a disadvantage too big to ignore. However, certain situations may mean that a sole proprietorship is the only option.

Partnership

A partnership is defined as "a formal arrangement by two or more parties to manage and operate a business and share its profits." (Kopp, C). Sharing in profits means that partners also share the liabilities. You do however get silent partners whose liability is limited due to their only contribution being financial. One could say that a partnership with no limited liability is like a sole proprietorship, but it is not only one person that takes on the liability.

You tend to find groups of professionals going into partnership and registering their business as a Limited Liability Partnership (LLP). Doctors or lawyers, for instance, would fit into this category, and one of the larger reasons for operating as an LLP is the possibility of malpractice lawsuits. Let's take a partnership made up of five doctors that share a medical clinic; if one of those doctors botches a procedure and is sued by the patient, and the partnership is not registered with limited liability, all five doctors will share the liability, should the lawsuit be successful.

Tax wise, an LLP is subject to pass-through tax, just like an S-Corp, meaning that partners are taxed in their personal capacity.

I certainly would not recommend a sole proprietorship or partnership above LLCs, C-Corps, and S-Corps, but on the taxation note, I would like to move to salaries, and how they are dealt with in S-Corps.

Reasonable Salaries

As an owner or group of owners, you want your salaries to be as low as possible, without being unreasonable. You can't pay salaries that are unlivable and put personal expenses through your business. Court cases have shown that the salaries must reflect the value of work done by the shareholder/s. Actual personal expenses must be taken into account, but perhaps you are in a situation where your spouse makes enough money to cover your total household expenses. Unfortunately, this doesn't mean that you can draw a minimal salary unless, of course, your value to the S-Corp is equivalent to a low salary. You need to look at the context because every situation is different, but you don't want to get the IRS to start asking questions.

How to Determine What a Reasonable Salary Is

An S-Corp can disguise remuneration as income distribution payments, but that isn't a wise idea, even though it is not strictly illegal. Your salary determination should be factual.

Realistic Compensation

The IRS will scrutinize shareholder-employee compensation. Bear in mind that non-salary distributions by an S-Corp are not taxable as part of payroll taxes. If the IRS does discover distribution payments, they have the power to reclassify the payments as wage payments, which means that they are subject to employment taxes. The reason I say that it is not illegal is that the form of wage payment is actually irrelevant. The declaration and correct classification on your returns is the relevant part. It is still disingenuous to purposefully mislabel wage payments. Once the IRS has done one reallocation, your S-Corp will be flagged, and if the information becomes public, it could cause reputational damage. It should not become public, but often confidentiality is broken.

Consider the scenario of an S-Corporation shareholder-employee named Alex. The IRS closely examines the compensation received by shareholder-employees like Alex. It's crucial to understand that distributions made by the S-Corp, which are not in the form of a salary, are not subject to payroll taxes.

However, if the IRS detects non-salary distributions that should have been classified as wages, they possess the authority to reclassify them as such. This means that the reclassified payments become subject to employment taxes.

It's important to note that the legality of the wage payment form is not the central issue; rather, accurate declaration and classification on tax returns are paramount. Deliberately mislabeling wage payments is not only disingenuous but can also have consequences. If the IRS reallocates payments once, the S-Corp may be flagged for closer scrutiny. If this information were to become public, it could potentially lead to reputational damage. While confidentiality is generally maintained, instances of it being breached are not unheard of.

Officers and Shareholders

There has been litigation challenging the IRS ruling that S-Corp payments to shareholders should be classified in terms of status as officer and shareholder, as opposed to the current classification as an employee. This is unlikely to change, but it is something to keep updated on. After all, you need to know the laws governing your S-Corp and the possibility of those laws being amended.

Family-provided Services

The IRS "punishes" family members for "working for free," or for doing work for the S-Corp and not being adequately compensated. The reason behind a family member assisting and not getting paid may be that the family has other assets that provide remuneration to that family member, such as a real estate portfolio. The IRS will have to determine what a reasonable payment for the services rendered would amount to and allocate tax accordingly. To be clear, a family member is defined by the IRS regulations as "the shareholder's spouse, ancestors, lineal descendants, and any trust of the primary benefit of any of these individuals" (Regs. Sec. 1.1366-3).

What Is Reasonable?

The IRS doesn't specifically define the term "reasonable," but it relies on the gross compensation received by shareholders and non-shareholders as employees for services. The other considerations are capital and equipment. Gross compensation receipts as a result of services rendered by non-shareholder employees, as well as capital and equipment are classified as non-wage distributions to the S-Corp shareholders, meaning that they are not subject to employment taxes.

However, if gross compensation receipts are generated by shareholders for direct personal services, they are considered wages and become taxable as employment taxes. If a shareholder-employee offers internal administrative services, such services will not directly produce determinable receipts. For example, if the shareholder employee trains staff in income-generating activities, which the staff then implement, and which in turn create day-to-day receipts, that shareholder is subject to tax on the receipts generated.

The IRS uses certain factors more than others when making a determination of what is reasonable; here are the main factors:

- when bonuses are paid, to whom, and in what manner

- specific compensation contracts/agreements

- how much experience employees have (how specialized their role/s are)

- what the industry-standard compensation is for the job or service provided

- the S-Corps history of dividend payments

- salary payments compared to amounts of profit distributed

- time dedicated to services to the S-Corp

- duties and responsibilities

Some Hypothetical Numbers

Below is a table with four different examples. The figures are hypothetical, and there is a comparison between a partnership and S-Corps. The percentage savings at the end are what you should focus on because a percentage doesn't change, but actual money/figures do. To explain the table, there is a comparison between a partnership and three salary categories. The fixed amounts for example are revenue, expenses, and profit prior to salaries. The comparison comes in from that point downwards, and the explanation percentage wise follows the table.

	Partner	High Salary	Medium Salary	Low Salary
Revenue per annum	400,000	400,000	400,000	400,000

Expenses per annum	50,000	50,000	50,000	50,000
Profit before salary per annum	350,000	350,000	350,000	350,000
Owner salary per annum	0	250,000	150,000	75,000
Company payroll taxes per annum	0	12,314.80	10,414.80	5,737.50
Profit per annum	350,000	87,685.20	189,585.20	269,262.50
Company payroll taxes brought down	0	12,314.80	10,414.80	5,737.50
Employer payroll taxes brought down	0	12,314.80	10,414.80	5,737.50
Self-employment	27,129	0	0	0

tax per annum				
Total tax per annum	27,129	24,629.20	20,829.50	11,475
Tax savings per annum	0	2,499.60	6,299.40	15,654

The high salary section leaves only $87,685.20 that does not attract payroll tax, meaning that when compared with a partnership, the tax-saving is 2.9%. Once salaries are kept below the $132,900 mark, the tax-saving benefits are worthwhile for an S-Corp. As before, the salaries have got to be reflective of the work contributions to the business. Highly qualified people such as doctors earn way more than $132,900, and the IRS would raise a red flag if they came across tax returns reflecting much lower salaries than reasonably possible. However, your company may be a high turnover, small profit business, and thus salaries are lower, meaning that the IRS would not raise a red flag at all.

My advice would be to sit with a tax specialist or accountant to go through projected figures on a table similar to the one above before making a decision. Don't lose sight of the limited liability benefit because a small saving might not be worth a lawsuit.

How to Run Payroll

Your salaries have to be structured, even if you are a one-person S-Corp. Technically you can't just take money out of your S-Corp whenever you want to. If you do, however, the IRS will most probably reallocate arbitrary withdrawals for tax purposes. From the table and explanation above, it should be clear that (depending on salary) profits above your salary are taxed at a lower rate.

Use Payroll Services

You will have to pay a monthly fee to a company that offers payroll services, and those services will make things a lot easier. A few days prior to payday, your payroll service will deduct the relevant amount from your business cheque/current account. When payday arrives, you and all other employees will receive your salaries as a payment into your respective personal accounts.

Qualified Business Income (QBI) Deduction

A new tax ruling came out in 2018, allowing business owners to claim a 20 percent deduction on QBI. Salaries that are paid to yourself as part of your S-Corp remuneration allowances do not count, meaning that your QBI deduction will drop quite significantly compared to using a partnership as your business vehicle. I have used the same revenue, expenses, and profit figures as in the table above for the sake of simplicity and only a high salary example to be prudent.

	Partner	High Salary
Revenue per annum	400,000	400,000
Expenses per annum	50,000	50,000

Profit before salary	350,000	350,000
Owner salary	0	250,000
Company payroll taxes per annum	0	12,314.80
Profit per annum	350,000	87,685.20
Qualified business income deduction per annum	70,000	17,537.04

Again, I would advise that you get a tax expert or accountant involved to give you assistance. Paying charges for the correct advice will save money in the long run.

Retirement Plan Options

Retirement Plan Options in the context of S-Corporations present a scenario where the allowable contributions are notably constrained, particularly when adopting the low salary approach. Unlike partnerships and sole proprietorships, where contributions are determined based on the total income, S-Corps impose more stringent limitations on retirement planning.

In S-Corps, the flexibility to contribute to retirement plans becomes limited, especially for those who opt for a lower salary structure. This constraint arises from the fact that the contribution calculations are intricately tied to the salary levels of the shareholders. Consequently, individuals within S-Corporations need to navigate these restrictions carefully when planning for their retirement, taking into account the unique considerations and limitations imposed by the corporate structure.

Suppose Mary is a shareholder-employee in an S-Corporation, and she decides to adopt a lower salary to optimize the distribution of profits. In this scenario, the allowable contributions to her retirement plan would be constrained due to the lower salary base.

Now, compare this with John, who operates a sole proprietorship. In his case, the retirement plan contributions are calculated based on the total income generated by the business. This grants John more flexibility in contributing to his retirement plan compared to Mary in the S-Corporation, as Mary's contributions are directly tied to her chosen salary level.

The distinction emphasizes that, in the context of retirement planning, S-Corporation shareholders may face limitations in contribution options, particularly when opting for a lower salary structure, as compared to their counterparts in sole proprietorships or partnerships.

Salaries From Other Sources

If you do have a full-time or even half-day job at which you earn a salary, but you are also a shareholder in an S-Corp, the likelihood of paying more taxes is high. However, it is unlikely that you would give up a permanent job to save on tax in your S-Corp, so it is a double-edged sword. Don't lose sight of the fact that employment contracts often preclude employees from earning outside income, so read your contract before making a commitment to an S-Corp.

Let's say that your salaried income is $275,000, and you are paid $50,000 from your S-Corp. Your self-employment tax will be at 2.9%. The reason is that you earn less than the $132,900 cap on your S-Corp income. But the S-Corp will have to pay the full percentage tax rate of 15.3% on your salary, and when you submit your tax return, you can only recover half of that in excess payroll taxes.

This scenario is probably not the best one to be in, but you have to work with actual figures, not just examples, to assess the viability.

S-Corp Versus C-Corp

Comparing these two entities will make your decision easier. The fundamental difference between the two is tax. S-Corps, as we know, are subject to pass-through tax. However, C-Corps are taxed as corporations. There are other differences, and at the outset, you need to know that C-Corps, in most situations, are used by large, staff-heavy entities that trade internationally and rely on foreign investment. That is not to say smaller businesses can't register as C-Corps, so let's have a look at the differences.

Ownership Options

Earlier in the book, I set out the options available to an S-Corp, but they differ when looking at registering a C-Corp. The former can have 100 shareholders or less, one stock class, and no foreign ownership. The latter may have unlimited shareholders, multiple classes of stock, and foreign ownership.

Limited Liability Protection

Limited Liability Protection is a critical aspect shared by both S-Corporations (S-Corps) and C-Corporations (C-Corps), offering individuals a substantial level of personal security and peace of mind. This legal principle ensures that the personal assets of the shareholders, directors, and officers are safeguarded from the business's debts and liabilities.

In the context of S-Corporations and C-Corporations, this means that in the event of legal actions, financial difficulties, or other challenges faced by the business, the personal assets of the individuals associated with the corporation remain shielded. Creditors and legal claimants typically cannot pursue the personal bank accounts, homes, or other possessions of shareholders or officers to satisfy the company's debts.

This limited liability protection is a fundamental advantage for individuals involved in corporate structures, as it separates personal and business finances, mitigating the potential impact of business-related issues on personal wealth. It provides individuals with a sense of security and confidence to engage in entrepreneurial activities, knowing that their personal assets are generally not at risk due to the business operations.

Pass-Through versus Corporate Tax

This is dependent on the size of your entity, but pass-through tax is a big plus in an S-Corp. Also, don't lose sight of the fact that the C-Corp tax rate is 21%, which is very high. However, the actual monetary tax amount will differ depending on the taxable amount.

Dealing With Losses

As we know, S-Corps can declare losses to offset shareholder income, whereas that option is not open to C-Corps. Many businesses run at losses, and in fact, the popular opinion is that a new business is likely to run at a loss for the first three years. Obviously, a loss is non-taxable, and you do get cases where accountants fiddle with the figures to reflect losses. NEVER do this; it really is not worth going to jail for bending tax laws.

Profit Distribution

With S-Corps, distribution is according to shareholding, based on the one class of stock requirement. C-Corps are not restricted in any way and may distribute profits by dividends, as well as by issuing shares. The latter is useful in attracting investors, and the flexibility assists in the credibility of the C-Corp.

Let's delve into an example to illustrate the dynamics of profit distribution in S-Corporations (S-Corps) and C-Corporations (C-Corps):

Consider two companies—Alpha Tech, an S-Corp, and Beta Industries, a C-Corp. Both companies have generated $1 million in profits for the fiscal year.

In Alpha Tech, an S-Corp, the profit distribution is directly tied to the shareholding of its shareholders. For instance, if there are two shareholders, Alex and Blake, each holding 50% of the shares, the $1 million profit would be distributed equally, with $500,000 going to Alex and $500,000 to Blake. This distribution structure is in line with the one class of stock requirement for S-Corps, ensuring fairness and simplicity in profit sharing among shareholders.

Now, let's turn to Beta Industries, a C-Corp. Unlike S-Corps, C-Corps have more flexibility in profit distribution. Beta Industries may choose to distribute profits through dividends, issuing shares, or a combination of both. This flexibility allows Beta Industries to attract investors by issuing additional shares, thus enhancing its capital base. Additionally, the ability to distribute profits via dividends or share issuance contributes to the credibility of Beta Industries as a corporate entity.

In summary, the example highlights the structured and shareholding-dependent profit distribution in S-Corps, in contrast to the versatile and investor-attractive mechanisms available to C-Corps.

S-Corp Suitability

- when you want to draw profits as income

- when you are able to benefit from losses

- to have a low personal income tax rate

- when you want to actively participate in day-to-day running

C-Corp Suitability

- when you have a foreign interest or want to pitch your business to potential overseas investors

- if you want to reinvest profit

- if you want unlimited growth potential (more than 100 shareholders)

- if you want different types of shareholders, such as trusts, other C-Corps, or international equivalents to U.S. corporates

- if you have owners with high personal tax rates

- if you want to attract local investors as well as foreign investors

Chapter Summary

There are different types of businesses, which means that business structures vary across different types of businesses. For example, a doctor or group of doctors is unlikely to structure its business in the same way that a logistics company does.

Money is a big deciding factor, and looking at actual figures is a good way to get valid information in order to make the decision as to whether an S-Corp is best suited to your business.

The lack of limited liability in sole proprietorships leaves the sole proprietor open to liability for all assets used in business activities or private activities. New business owners are sometimes left with no choice but to operate as sole proprietors due to limited funds, but the option to register an LLC or S-Corp at a later stage is always there.

Partnerships are not advisable because liability is not limited. A partnership can be registered as a Limited Liability Partnership (LLP), which is most often used by professionals, such as accountants or lawyers.

Salary amounts are impacted by the tax, depending on thresholds. For instance, a salary below the cap of $132,900 attracts a tax rate of 2.9%. However, the IRS requires that salaries are in proportion to work done or the value of the business. Take the doctor example; a doctor is worth way more than $132,900, and if that doctor was drawing a salary under the cap, the IRS is likely to have questions. The two tables with figures set out in this chapter should be very useful in calculating the best financial structure. Retirement plans are important, and S-Corps restrict contributions, so you have to weigh up the factors, including this one.

It is possible to have a salary from a job and still be a shareholder who draws a salary from an S-Corp. This is dangerous territory and could result in higher overall taxation.

An alternative to an S-Corp is a C-Corp, both of which have advantages and disadvantages, and overlaps. Both have limited liability, but S-Corps have restrictions as to the number of shareholders and are not allowed to have overseas shareholders.

C-Corps are much less restrictive, as they have unlimited shareholding options and are permitted to have foreign investors. This doesn't mean that C-Corps are an automatic best choice; it is a subjective choice depending on your business type. If you want to reinvest profit, issue multiple stock shares, and you want to attract investors, then a C-Corp is the way to go. If you want to draw benefits from losses and also draw profits, in addition to minimizing tax, then an S-Corp is your answer.

Don't forget that the money side of the decision should be explored with a tax expert or accountant, and do remember that a fee for such professional advice will probably save you money when your business is fully operational.

At this point, you should have a more specific understanding of S-Corps and an understanding of their suitability for your business. It is time to continue onto the actual formation of your S-Corp and the steps that you need to take to do so.

CHAPTER 12
STARTING YOUR S-CORP

You have made your decision, and you are ready to get going. This chapter will guide you through the steps required and give advice on what to do within each step to make the process as easy as possible. There is, of course, the option of appointing an expert in the field, and as I have said before and will say again, money spent on such will very likely save money in the long run.

Step 1: Decide on a Unique Name for Your Business

A name should get across what the business actually does. Avoid meaningless titles like CRF Services or BTR Proprietors, or Hanson Brothers. Rather choose a name such as CRF Accounting Services if your business is an accounting firm. BTR Real Estate Proprietors if your business is an estate agency and Hanson Brothers Furniture if your business is a furniture retailer.

Example: GreenHarvest Organics

In this case, "GreenHarvest Organics" effectively communicates the nature of your business—organic farming. The name combines elements that are associated with eco-friendliness and the agricultural sector, making it both meaningful and memorable. This choice aligns with the recommendation to avoid generic or abstract names, ensuring that potential clients or customers can easily understand what your business does.

Step 2: Check if the Name is Not Already Taken by Another Business

You don't want your name to sound similar or be exactly the same as an existing business. Most businesses have an online presence, so use Google to search your proposed names and see if your business name will clash with others. You might want to go for a cheesy pun or something that rhymes or a different take on spelling, in order to grab the attention of potential customers. Something like "Movers and Shakers Furniture Transport" or "No Shorts Electrical."

Step 3: Choose the State in Which You Intend to Form Your S-Corp

You should remember that in chapter 1, I listed the four states in which S-Corps do not have pass-through tax: Michigan, California, New Jersey, and New York. These states tax S-Corps as corporations, and the following states do not recognize S-Corps at all: Columbia, New Hampshire, and Tennessee. Most often, S-Corps will be registered in the state where they are domiciled. Domicile is the address from which your C-Corp trades.

If your S-Corp is completely online operated then Delaware is the best state in which to form the S-Corp. The process is the easiest out of all the states, the tax rates and tax benefits are very favorable, and the state offices are helpful and efficient.

Step 4: File and Submit the S-Corp's Articles of Association/ Incorporation

Below is an example of what articles of incorporation will look like. You can draft and complete the document yourself, but using a professional will eliminate possible errors.

ARTICLES OF INCORPORATION OF:

ABC FURNITURE REMOVALS

Under the Business Corporation Laws of the state of Delaware.

The name of the corporation is ABC Furniture Removals.

The principal place of incorporation is _____

The name and address of the registered agent is _____

The purpose for which the incorporation is organized is

_____

The corporation is authorized to issue X amount of shares:

Without a par value of ____ or without a par value (2022) .

Names and addresses of all directors are as follows (legaltemplates, n.d.):

_____

_____

Names and addresses of all financial officers are as follows (legaltemplates, n.d.):

_____

_____

The name and address of the incorporator is:

_____

The period of duration of the corporation is (legaltemplates, n.d.):

Perpetual or X number of years or ends on X date.

Executed, signed, and witnessed on the X date of X month, X year.

_____

Signature of shareholder/s

_____

Witness signature

Step 5: Determine the Board of Directors

The board of directors can comprise all of the shareholders or some of the shareholders, and the limit is 100 individuals. It is very unlikely that every single one of the 100 shareholders will be a member of the board of directors in an instance where there is such a vast number of shareholders, but it is possible.

Step 6: Keep Minutes of all Shareholder Meetings and Board Meetings

When any decision affecting the running of the S-Corp is made, it needs to be recorded by the shareholders, and/or board of directors in an officially chaired meeting. The meeting need not be formal or lengthy as long as the important and prevalent parts of the meeting are noted and recorded.

Let's consider a scenario for an S-Corporation named "TechInnovate Solutions" to illustrate the importance of keeping minutes for shareholder and board meetings.

Example: Minutes of a Shareholder Meeting at TechInnovate Solutions

Date: January 15, 202X

Location: TechInnovate Solutions Headquarters

Present:

John Smith (Shareholder)

Emily Jones (Shareholder)

Sarah Davis (Board Member)

Michael Chen (Board Member)

Lisa Rodriguez (Chairperson)

Agenda Items:

Financial Update:

John presented the financial report for the last quarter.

Shareholders discussed and approved the financial statement.

Strategic Planning:

Sarah proposed a new marketing strategy for Q2.

Shareholders provided input and reached a consensus on the strategy.

Board Elections:

Lisa announced the upcoming board elections.

Shareholders discussed the nomination process and set a timeline.

Key Decisions:

Unanimous approval of the financial statement.

Adoption of the proposed marketing strategy.

Agreement on the timeline for board elections.

Note: While the meeting was informal, all key decisions and discussions were recorded to ensure transparency and compliance with S-Corporation governance requirements. Keeping minutes serves as an official record of decisions made during the meeting and provides a reference for future actions.

Step 7: Get an Employer Identification Number (EIN) and File a Form 2553 to Elect S-Corp Tax Status

An EIN is your Employer Identification Number, which you will obtain on application from the IRS. When you have been allocated your EIN, you will need to complete form 2553. The form can be downloaded from the IRS website or obtained from your local IRS office. It is the form on which you apply for shareholders to be subject to individual tax.

There is some repetition from the articles of association across form 2553, but for the sake of completeness, this is the information required on form 2553:

- The name of your business

- The physical address of your business

- Your EIN

- The state in which you wish your S-Corp to be registered in

- The date of incorporation

- The effective date of the S-Corp election

- A complete list of all shareholder information

- A comprehensive set of information on your fiscal tax year

- All shareholders signatures

You will also require a witness to the signatures. An outside party can be a witness, but nobody involved in the set-up of the S-Corp can act as a witness. An employee or non-shareholder is permitted to be a witness, and do remember that the witness is a witness to the signature and nothing else.

A Look at the Two Main Ways to Set Up an S-Corp

LLC

Form an LLC first, then select your S-Corp tax status from the IRS, after which, request your Employer Identification Number (EIN). The steps to set up an LLC are very similar to the steps to set up an S-Corp, so I am not going to go into great detail. Here they are, in shortened form, followed by the three types of conversions:

- Choose the name

- Check that the name is available

- Choose the state

- Appoint a registered agent

- Fill in and file the articles of organization (almost the same as articles of association)

- Prepare and file the form

- Draw up an operating agreement

My advice is if you intend using this method, you should try to get both forms and fill them in at the same time, with professional assistance.

Statutory Conversion

Depending on your state, you can do a "quick-status" conversion, in which you will fill in the forms, and submit them to the secretary of state. The time periods are short, and as the name suggests, the status change does not take long.

Statutory Merger Information

This option gives you the chance to merge your existing LLC into a new corporation. First, you will create the new corporation and then have a vote involving LLC members for approval to change the members to shareholders. If this is a decision, it will be made as a group, so the election could very well be simple, hands up for yes, count the votes, hands up for no and count the votes. The final step is to file a certificate of merger, available from the office of the secretary of state or the IRS website.

Non-statutory Conversion

You will require lawyers and accountants if you use this method, which can make it expensive. It is also a complicated process, as you are required to create the corporation and then transfer any assets and liabilities that your existing LLC has in its name, and then liquidate the LLC, and dissolve it.

C-Corp

C-Corps differ from LLCs and S-Corps, more than S-Corps differ from LLCs, but I will still go into the relevant details. Naming your business and checking that the name is available remains the same.

Next, you need to arrange your leadership by appointing shareholders and directors. Then, file the articles of association and issue stock certificates. Finally, apply for the requisite business licenses and/or permits. When all the paperwork is done, you can then convert to an S-Corp.

Using a Company to Create Your S-Corp

I have mentioned previously that hiring a tax expert or an accountant would be a good idea, but using a single company to do everything as a one-stop shop is probably the easiest way to do it. As with any commercial service, costs vary greatly, but cheap and expensive are relative to your budget or the budget of your S-Corp. I have compiled a list of ten companies through experience and research. My choices are based on the most user-friendly website, the quality of the service, and whether or not the fees are reasonable. The list is in no particular order, and all of the companies are easily findable with a simple Google search.

- Offshore Company Corp

- Delaware Inc.

- Three Point O

- Swyft Filings

- Doola.com

- First Base

- Up Counsel

- Globalization Partners

- My Corporation

- My Company Works

On the question of fees, you will notice that several of the above companies state just their fee on their website but do not include fees payable to the state registering authority. Other companies state the full price, which includes their fee and the registration fees with the state department. Be aware of these factors when you are exploring and deciding which service to go with.

Financing Your S-Corp

Nobody likes to create debt, and doing so can be a source of tremendous stress and worry. However, sometimes it can be inevitable, and other than the set-up costs of an S-Corp in terms of registration, you may need to put deposits down for office rental, furniture, equipment, and other unavoidable costs. Banks and financiers often have credit plans specifically for new businesses.

To work out how much money you require upfront, you should make lists of exactly what you need and the costs thereof, get to a final figure, and then put on a 20% contingency for any unforeseen costs. It is a good idea to put together a complete business plan, with the numbers on a spreadsheet, so when you approach an institution for finance, they can see that you have your ducks in a row and that you intend to succeed.

Banks don't (shouldn't) dish out loans to anyone, so the impression that you make on behalf of your S-Corp is very important.

Every year Forbes puts out a list of business financiers with ratings of four and five out of five stars. It is definitely worth having a look at these lists and deciding on which institution will work best for you. There is another option, which I would argue is the best one, and that is the lending marketplace, which does not restrict you to one institution. If you have a range of options that are easily attainable, it can only benefit your power of choice.

Business Lending Marketplace

What follows are five essentials that any businessperson interested in financing a new business or giving an existing business a cash injection needs to know. Don't just brush over these; they are vital in planning financially.

You Are Not Restricted to One Option

Let's say hypothetically that you want to buy a car. You are not going to walk into the first dealership, pick one out and buy it. Most people will look around, go to more than one dealership and find the best deal. The same should apply to finding a business loan.

A lending marketplace allows you to compare loan amounts, repayment periods, interest rates, and the amount of time it takes to have a loan approved. It is a bit like using a site that allows you to book flights across multiple airlines based on all the information on that one site. Don't lose sight of the fact that cheaper may not always be beneficial, do your homework properly.

Flexibility

Your S-Corp may be in a position where it will require a short-term loan to make a bulk stock payment in order to take advantage of a rebate from a supplier, or you may need to take a long-term loan to set up your infrastructure. Being able to choose from a variety of options gives you the tools to find the best lending strategy for what you specifically require.

Time-Saving

You do not have to fill out an application for every single credit provider. A lending marketplace allows access to offers from several lenders. All you have to do is complete the necessary forms online and hit the submit button. For example, Lendio.com works with over 75 lenders, and if you approached each one individually, it would take weeks, maybe months.

Expert Guidance

The teams on lending marketplace websites are trained and qualified to answer any questions that you may have. You don't have to restrict yourself to just one lending marketplace before you make decisions that best suit your S-Corp.

Speed and Size

Sometimes you need a small loan fast. Other times you may be looking for a larger loan, and you have more time to explore options. With a small loan, the interest rate may not be that important, but rather fast access to money may be the main deciding factor. When looking for a larger loan, you will probably have more time to explore different options, especially when it comes to the interest rates.

Types of Loans

As touched on previously, different businesses require different types of loans. Here are some options to be aware of.

Business Line Credit Option

This is a type of loan that you only use when you actually need to. It is available all the time, set to a limit, depending on what you qualify for. It can lay dormant for six months if you don't require its use, but you can draw on it quickly if you require cash for whatever business purpose. You only pay interest on what you use. Repayment terms and plans differ from credit provider to credit provider, which is another reason to use lending marketplaces to make a decision.

Consider a small retail business, "Sunshine Gifts," that experiences seasonal fluctuations in cash flow. They opt for a Business Line of Credit to address occasional working capital needs.

Scenario:

Sunshine Gifts qualifies for a $50,000 line of credit from a lending institution.

The business decides to keep the credit line dormant during the slower months when cash flow is steady.

As the holiday season approaches and they anticipate increased sales, Sunshine Gifts taps into the line of credit to purchase additional inventory.

They draw $20,000 from the credit line, using it to stock up on popular holiday merchandise.

Key Points:

The Business Line of Credit remains available throughout the year, providing flexibility.

Sunshine Gifts only pays interest on the $20,000 utilized for inventory expansion.

Repayment terms are tailored to fit the business's cash flow, ensuring manageable payments.

This example illustrates how a Business Line of Credit offers businesses the flexibility to access funds when needed, aligning with their unique cash flow patterns and specific financial requirements.

Small Business Loans

A small business loan is finite in that it has a specific term, a specific interest rate, or an interest rate linked to the prime lending rate, and is for a specific amount of time. This is the original type of business loan that has existed since banks began lending money. Your decision in this instance will be based not necessarily on how many shareholders you have, but on the size of the business relative to setup costs.

Imagine a start-up named "TechLaunch Innovations," founded by two entrepreneurs, Alex and Sarah. They need initial capital to set up their tech development firm and decide to explore Small Business Loans.

Scenario:

"TechLaunch Innovations" applies for a small business loan of $100,000 from a local bank.

The loan has a fixed term of three years and an interest rate of 5% linked to the prime lending rate. The funds are intended for equipment purchase, office space lease, and initial marketing efforts. Alex and

Sarah carefully consider the loan terms and monthly repayments to ensure alignment with their business's size and projected income.

Key Points:

The Small Business Loan provides a specific amount of capital for a set purpose.

The loan's finite term and interest rate are clearly defined at the outset.

Repayment is structured over the designated three-year period.

This example showcases how a Small Business Loan, with its well-defined terms and purpose, can serve as a foundational financing option for startups like "TechLaunch Innovations" to cover initial setup costs and establish a solid financial footing.

Business Cash Advance

Any loan has a form of risk attached to it, but this one carries substantial risk. A business cash advance requires future collateral that is provided via profit projections. Once you are granted your advance, the pressure is on, but at the end of the day, you want to make money, so maybe the pressure is a good thing.

Let's consider a scenario for a restaurant owner named Mark who is seeking quick funds to renovate his establishment. Facing a time-sensitive opportunity, Mark decides to explore a Business Cash Advance.

Scenario:

Mark applies for a Business Cash Advance of $30,000 to revamp his restaurant's interior and expand the menu.

The advance is approved based on the business's projected profits, and repayment is tied to a percentage of future credit card sales.

Mark receives the funds quickly, enabling him to initiate the renovation project immediately.

As the renovation progresses, Mark strategically promotes the changes, attracting more customers and increasing sales.

Key Points:

The Business Cash Advance is based on future collateral, utilizing profit projections.

Repayment is directly linked to the business's credit card sales, providing flexibility.

The pressure to succeed and generate revenue becomes a driving force for Mark to maximize the business's potential.

This example illustrates how a Business Cash Advance, while carrying inherent risks, can serve as a valuable financing tool for business owners like Mark, especially in situations where time-sensitive opportunities demand swift access to capital.

Equipment Financing

Whether you need a tractor, an industrial dishwasher, or a set of smart tables and chairs for your boardroom, you can apply to finance that equipment. Now, remember that if you do not make your repayments, the equipment may be subject to repossession.

I hope at this stage you are thinking back to the limiting of liability, and you would be right to do so. Sometimes there is no choice but to put assets purchased into the S-Corps name, but when you take this option, be very careful to make sure that you will meet the repayments.

Let's consider a scenario for a landscaping business called "GreenScape Services" that needs to acquire a new tractor for its operations. The business explores Equipment Financing to facilitate the purchase.

Scenario:

"GreenScape Services" applied for Equipment Financing to acquire a specialized tractor costing $50,000.

The financing is approved, and the business secures the necessary funds with a fixed interest rate and repayment terms spanning five years.

The new tractor enhances the efficiency of landscaping operations, contributing to increased productivity and client satisfaction.

Key Points:

Equipment Financing provides a tailored solution for acquiring specific business assets.

The financing terms are structured based on the cost and lifespan of the equipment.

"GreenScape Services" carefully manages repayments to avoid any risk of equipment repossession.

This example showcases how Equipment Financing allows businesses to acquire essential assets, such as specialized machinery, while emphasizing the importance of meeting repayment obligations to prevent any adverse impact on the acquired equipment or the business's financial stability.

Business Start-up Loan

This type of loan will most likely not require collateral, although that is not the case in every situation. It is what it is called and is used to start up a new business from the ground up.

Consider a scenario where an aspiring entrepreneur named Alex is passionate about launching a boutique coffee shop called "Bean Haven" in a bustling city neighborhood. To turn this dream into reality, Alex explores the option of a Business Start-up Loan.

Scenario:

Alex applies for a Business Start-up Loan of $80,000 from a local lending institution to cover initial expenses.

The loan, granted based on Alex's business plan and creditworthiness, carries a competitive interest rate.

"Bean Haven" utilizes the funds to secure a suitable location, purchase coffee brewing equipment, and cover initial marketing costs.

With the financial support from the Business Start-up Loan, "Bean Haven" opens its doors, attracting coffee enthusiasts and establishing a presence in the community.

Key Points:

Business Start-up Loans are tailored for entrepreneurs initiating new ventures.

Collateral may not be a requirement in many cases, making it accessible to startups.

The loan enables entrepreneurs like Alex to bring their business vision to life from the ground up.

This example illustrates how a Business Start-up Loan serves as a crucial financial tool for aspiring entrepreneurs to turn their business ideas into reality, providing the necessary capital to cover initial expenses and establish a strong foundation for the new venture.

Short-Term Loan

This kind of credit is best suited to situations when your S-Corp needs money and needs it fast. A short-term loan is processed in a few minutes and often pays out within 24 hours. Generally, full payment is required within a specified period. So let's say a supplier has offered you an upfront payment discount, and you have a buyer for the product but are short on cash. Then you take the loan out, buy the stock, sell it and repay the loan with the proceeds of the sale. A short-term loan can be used to your advantage in a situation like the above.

Commercial Mortgage

If you want to buy the premises from which you will be operating your business, a mortgage is the way to go. Very few new businesses or even existing businesses can afford to buy immovable property in cash. One specific advantage is that as time goes by and you start creating equity in the S-Corp's property, you can borrow further to do renovations or additions.

Imagine a growing manufacturing company named "TechForge Industries" that has been leasing its production facility for several years. With plans to expand and secure a permanent location, they opt for a Commercial Mortgage.

Scenario:

"TechForge Industries" decides to purchase a 10,000 square foot industrial property for $1 million to serve as its permanent manufacturing facility.

The company applies for a Commercial Mortgage with a reputable lender, securing a loan with a fixed interest rate and a 20-year repayment term.

The mortgage allows "TechForge Industries" to acquire the property and transition from leasing to owning their operational premises.

Over the years, as the company builds equity in the property, they consider borrowing additional funds against the property to finance renovations and facility improvements.

Key Points:

Commercial Mortgages are instrumental in facilitating the purchase of business premises.

They provide an avenue for businesses to acquire property without the need for substantial upfront cash.

The built equity in the property allows for potential future borrowings to support business expansion and improvements.

This example demonstrates how a Commercial Mortgage serves as a strategic financing solution for businesses like "TechForge Industries," enabling them to transition from leasing to ownership and leverage property equity for further business enhancements.

Accounts Receivable Financing

I would not advise any business to take this option. Basically, the financier will pay your S-Corp a percentage of your customer invoices up front, usually somewhere around 80%, but when your customer/s pay the invoice, the financier takes a share. Usually, the share is 3–5%.

It seems good on principle, but whether or not your customers pay on time, late, or not at all, the financier will come running for their percentage very quickly. I'm not saying that this option doesn't work, but I see the risk as quite high. It does, of course, depend on the individual situation of the S-Corp, so in some instances, it may be riskier than others, but just be cautious on this one.

Small Business Administration Loan (SBA)

This is a business loan partially backed by the government. The SBA does not actually provide the cash but rather establishes guidelines for loans and provides guarantees for certain portions of those loans.

Consider a scenario where a family-owned bakery, "Sweet Beginnings," wishes to expand its operations by opening a second location. To fund this expansion, they explore the option of a Small Business Administration (SBA) Loan.

Scenario:

"Sweet Beginnings" applied for an SBA Loan of $150,000 from a local bank to support the establishment of a new bakery branch.

The SBA partially guarantees the loan, providing assurance to the lender and reducing the risk associated with the business expansion.

The loan funds are utilized for securing a suitable location, purchasing additional baking equipment, and covering initial marketing expenses.

With the support of the SBA Loan, "Sweet Beginnings" successfully opens its new bakery, attracting more customers and contributing to the growth of the family business.

Key Points:

SBA Loans are government-backed loans designed to support small businesses.

The SBA establishes guidelines and provides guarantees for portions of the loan to encourage lenders to extend credit.

"Sweet Beginnings" leverages the SBA Loan to achieve their expansion goals and strengthen their presence in the local market.

This example illustrates how a Small Business Administration Loan can empower small businesses like "Sweet Beginnings" to pursue expansion opportunities by providing crucial financial support and reducing the risk for lenders.

Operating Agreement

Now that we have looked at different ways for financing your business, it is time to look at something equally as essential; the operating agreement. An operating agreement is a legal document that outlines the internal workings, structure, and regulations of a company.

The operating agreement for an S Corporation should comprehensively detail all corporate bylaws and articles of incorporation. Prior to drafting corporate bylaws, conducting thorough research on the applicable state laws is crucial. This ensures a deeper understanding of potential legal considerations and issues that may be relevant to the corporation's operations within that specific jurisdiction.

It is wise to have an operating agreement, to manage expectations and make sure that all shareholders are absolutely clear on the important aspects of the business. Below is a sample of an operating agreement (Upcounsel, 2020). It is not too complicated to draw one up, and you can get templates on various free document sites.

Operating Agreement Between

XYZ S-Corp

And

Shareholder One

And

Shareholder Two

This operating agreement is entered into between Shareholder One and Shareholder Two, as members, and XYZ S-Corp, as the company, on the following terms:

The name of the business is XYZ S-Corp, and is situated at 123 First Avenue.

The purpose of the business is to operate lawfully as a Limited Liability S-Corp, as a furniture manufacturer and fitment business.

This agreement will take effect on X date and run indefinitely, until such time as the S-Corp is dissolved, for whatever reason whatsoever.

All certificates or documents requiring publication will be published after this agreement has been signed.

The members have agreed to each put forward $10,000 as start-up capital, the total being $20,000, as the total contribution from the two shareholders.

The annual net income or net loss shall be allocated to the members each fiscal year.

Members may sell, assign or transfer shareholding in the company, but not before written consent from the other shareholders.

If the shareholders resolve to dissolve the business, the members will take full account for the assets and liabilities of the company and will liquidate the assets within a reasonable time period and at an amount/s consistent with reasonable market value.

The business shall be member-managed.

Amendments will only be valid when placed in writing. This document comprises the entire operating agreement.

_____   _____

Signature of shareholder/s   *Signature of shareholder/s*

_____

Witness signature

Chapter Summary

When you have decided that you want to start an S-Corp, there are seven steps that you need to follow, as set out above. Choose a name that is not already taken, and that is not similar to an existing business and then pick the state in which you want to register your S-Corp. Draft your C-Corps Articles of Association, as per the example set out under step four. Establish your board of directors and from the first meeting, record everything discussed in every meeting. Apply for your employer identification number and when received, fill in form 2553, to elect your tax status.

Be aware of the information required on the said form, as per the bullet points under step seven, and the two main ways of setting an S-Corp, i.e., LLC conversion or C-Corp then to S-Corp. Consider an expert to take care of all the steps for you, and remember that paying an expert will probably save you money in the longer term, and ensure that the process runs smoothly. Pay attention to the ten listed companies that I recommended and jump on Google for more information on their services.

Financing is something to think about, and it is vital to arrive at a figure that covers absolutely everything, then add a contingency for miscellaneous expenses, and come to a grand total. From that point, you can explore which financing option is best for your S-Corp. Business lending marketplaces give you information on several loans and credit options, which you can access by doing just one application.

There is a diverse range of financing options, from the government-backed SBA loan system to commercial mortgages, if your S-Corp intends to buy offices or premises. When you are considering what will serve your S-Corp best, don't forget the importance of limited liability. I believe that this chapter will have given you peace of mind that you know how to get your S-Corp to the point of readiness to trade and that you have an understanding of choosing the correct set-up and financing route suited best to your S-Corp.

The final part of the chapter is an example of an operating agreement. It is a very simple one but gives you an accurate idea of what one looks like.

CHAPTER 13
WHAT NOT TO DO

I f you are starting a business for the very first time, the setup can be seen as a teaser to a movie, and the real start is your first day of trading. Things can go wrong, so let's take a dive into some advice about what not to do.

There are several reasons that businesses fail, and a sad fact is that already established businesses could not survive the economic restrictions that the COVID-19 pandemic imposed. In that sense, business closures were, and continue to be unavoidable.

If you have a relatively new business or are starting one soon, whether it is an S-Corp or not, you need to pay attention to taking care of the aspects that are within your control.

More than 18% of new businesses fail in the first two years, and more than 55% do not get past the five-year mark. By reading this book and taking note of what follows, the chances of your business succeeding are doubled, perhaps even tripled.

Mistakes to Avoid When Starting Your Business

Being Afraid to Fail

We hear this often (Schooley, 2022). There is a difference between being nervous and being afraid. Don't let thoughts of failure enter your mind. We also often hear the recommendation of having a plan B or not putting all your eggs in one basket.

However, if you only have a plan A, you have the motivation to succeed. There will be setbacks, no business that has ever existed has run smoothly all the time; it is just not possible. Expect that things will go wrong, but do not dwell on that. Do everything you can, and if you face a bump in the road, deal with it when it happens.

Not Making a Business Plan

The cheesy saying, *"failing to plan, is planning to fail,"* is so true. You can't just throw yourself into a project without knowing what you are doing. You will learn as you go, but having a comprehensive plan should allow you to do as much as you can from the get-go.

Being Disorganized

People seem to think that if you are disorganized, then that is that, but if you have a propensity for disorganization, it can be changed. Get a diary; keep physical files as well as electronic ones. Keep a diary, and don't leave tasks, do them immediately. Procrastination also falls into this category. Make sure you display organization and immediacy from day one of trading your S-Corp. It isn't that difficult!

Here are some specific organization tips tailored for starting an S Corporation (S-Corp):

Comprehensive Record-Keeping:

- Establish a meticulous record-keeping system for financial transactions, contracts, and important documents.

- Maintain both physical and digital copies for redundancy.

Immediate Task Handling:

- Cultivate a habit of addressing tasks promptly; don't leave them pending.

- Prioritize tasks related to S-Corp formation, tax obligations, and initial operations.

Strategic Use of Business Tools:

- Implement specialized S-Corp management tools for compliance and reporting.

- Explore accounting software tailored for S-Corps to streamline financial processes.

Tax Calendar and Reminders:

- Set up a tax calendar with key dates for S-Corp filings.

- Use reminders to ensure timely submission of required documents.

Structured Document Organization:

- Develop a filing system for essential S-Corp documents, such as the Articles of Incorporation, bylaws, and EIN paperwork.

- Clearly label folders for easy access.

Detailed Business Plan:

- Create a comprehensive business plan outlining goals, strategies, and financial projections.

- Regularly review and update the plan as your S-Corp evolves.

Clear Financial Tracking:

- Implement a robust financial tracking system to monitor income, expenses, and shareholder transactions.

- Use accounting software or hire a professional accountant for accuracy.

Scheduled Compliance Checks:

- Establish a regular schedule for compliance checks to ensure adherence to state regulations and federal requirements.

- Address any compliance issues promptly.

Shareholder Communication Strategy:

- Develop a communication strategy for regular updates and engagement with shareholders.

- Clearly outline roles and responsibilities within the S-Corp structure.

Employee Onboarding System:

- If hiring employees, establish an organized onboarding process.

- Ensure compliance with employment laws and document all necessary HR procedures.

Legal and Regulatory Research:

- Stay informed about legal requirements specific to S-Corps in your state.

- Regularly conduct legal research to address any changes in regulations.

Secure Digital Infrastructure:

- Implement secure digital practices for data storage and communication.

- Ensure cybersecurity measures are in place to protect sensitive information.

Regular Reporting Practices:

- Develop a routine for generating and reviewing financial reports.

- Share reports with stakeholders to maintain transparency.

Emergency Preparedness Plan:

- Establish an emergency preparedness plan for unforeseen events affecting S-Corp operations.

- Include contingency measures for key business functions.

Remember that organization is a fundamental aspect of S-Corp management, contributing to efficiency, compliance, and overall success. Adjust these tips based on the specific needs and structure of your S-Corp.

Not Defining Your Target Market

If you don't know who you are selling to then you are going to struggle to sell. You may have a very niche market. Let's say your S-Corp supplies a specialized type of heavy-duty screw used on 34-tonne trucks. That market is very specific, so you need to tailor advertising and marketing campaigns toward logistics companies and fleet owners. If you sell dishwashing liquid, your potential market is huge, but you need to be unique and reasonably priced. It is probably more difficult to sell dishwashing liquid than a specific type of hardware used in the trucking industry. You can include these details in your business plan, or you can develop a separate marketing plan.

Not Filing for the Appropriate Business Type/ Classification

What you have read up until now has given you all the knowledge and tools to get your S-Corp going, so at this point, you are aware that this is the correct type of business vehicle for your purposes.

Trying to Do Everything Yourself

Starting a business on your own can be intimidating, and while you should avoid thinking about failure, keep in mind that there are people who can assist you. Not necessarily with the actual running of your business, but with aspects of it. Our networks in this day and age are really big, and one can always find a friend of a friend who is willing to help.

Think about it like this; when (not if) you become a successful entrepreneur, it would be wonderful if you could help up-and-comers in your field. That means that there are successful people that are in such a position now. Paying experts to do something in a few days that would take you a week is something to consider. Perhaps your forte is sales, but you're not great at Excel. You could hire someone to work one morning a week, perhaps a retired accounting teacher who is looking for something to occupy themselves.

Getting the Wrong Investors

Without a doubt, there are people out there who will scam you and try and make a quick buck or investors that will put what looks like a great deal on the table, only for you to discover that it isn't that great after business commences. If it sounds too good to be true, it probably is (Schooley, 2022). Your business is like your child. You want to nurture it and guide it as it grows and begins to succeed. Only partner with people or institutions that have the same outlook. In the previous chapter, we looked at financiers, but those were bigger players in finance. I am talking about smaller investors. I'm not saying don't explore offers or opportunities, but on this one, it is very advisable to have a lawyer look over any contract before you put pen to paper.

Avoiding Contracts

A he said/she said situation can easily be prevented if you put everything down in writing. A so-called "gentlemen's agreement" may have business romanticism to it, but this is the time to be cynical. You can't make a supply deal over the phone and then fail to put the terms in writing thereafter. If something goes wrong, you are going to want to produce written proof in order to settle whatever disagreement may arise.

Hiring Too Soon

There must be a mix between doing everything yourself and hiring others to do so. A new business doesn't start with a decent cash flow in the first month, so do as much as you can with the time you have. The time to start hiring is when you become too busy to attend to every part of the running of your business. As I said, it is a mix, and some services you will have to pay for, even if you are not busy yet. Take the Excel example above and apply that to this tip as well.

Understanding Capital Requirements

As I said in the previous chapter, when you calculate your set-up costs, you need to build in a contingency. I suggest 20% because there will be unforeseen costs. For instance, you need an industrial printer, and you are under the impression that the ink is part of the cost. You discover that such is not the case, and now your budget is out, but not if you have built-in that contingency. You want to avoid going back to the bank or financier a second time to increase your start-up loan.

Wasting Money

Your product must be the best it can be, but you don't need brand-new hardwood furniture, a TV in the boardroom, and a fancy coffee machine. Those things can come later in your journey.

Focus on what is important, i.e., a good product or service and an effective marketing strategy.

Paying Yourself the Wrong Salary

You should remember the table in chapter 3, setting out a partnership versus an S-Corp, comparing low, medium, and high salaries. Refer back to that, as getting the salary correct, within a range of course, in order to minimize tax, is vital. Even if your business starts increasing its turnover rapidly, don't take too much money out. Rather, pay off your startup loan or other chosen financing.

Undervaluing or Overvaluing Your Product/Service

Among other things, your goal is to make money, but don't be greedy. If you are the most expensive product on the market, your product must be extremely unique and your service must be exceptional. Some companies do indeed use service as their draw card.

Also, don't cut your margins to an amount that will see to it that you have to sell way more of your product than is actually possible to make a decent amount of money. Investigate what your competitors are charging, do your homework, and set your pricing at a fair value. If people feel that they are getting fair value for money, that is when your product starts selling itself, and your quality of service is spread by word of mouth.

Launching Too Quickly

You need to check and double-check that all aspects of the business are ready before you launch. As an example, you have been talking to a potential customer about signing a supply contract when you launch, and everything seems to be on track. The contract is not yet signed, but it is the last thing that needs to be done before you can start to manufacture your product.

Even though the signature has not hit the page you decide to push play on the manufacture, which brings with it certain expenses. Your thinking is that by the time the product is ready, the contract will be signed, and your business will be off to a good start. You do a big launch and set the marketing wheels in motion, only to discover that the potential customer has gone with another supplier. So you sit with an excess of stock, which you have paid for, and nobody to sell it to.

The point is that you need to make sure everything is in place before you launch. This is just an example of many possibilities. As I said before, things do go wrong, but as I also said, control the things that you can control. It is understandable that the emotions associated with that first deal may tempt you to press go before you are ready, but hang on until you really are ready.

Expanding Too Quickly

If you experience initial success, which I hope you do, that doesn't mean that you need to hire a bunch of staff straight away and move to bigger premises. Expansion should come when you and your fellow shareholders do not have time to attend to everything required in running a successful business. Your balance sheet is also important, in that if you can employ someone to take care of managing manufacture, to allow you to get out into the market and attend to the promoting and selling of your product, in order to make more money, then the time for expansion has come.

Don't fall into the trap of securing one contract and having grandiose ideas of immediate economic growth, then hiring a bunch of people that may end up sitting around half the day. Expanding does not only refer to taking on staff but also to taking on tasks that your fledgling business does not have the capabilities of doing just yet.

Hypothetically, you distribute chipboard used in the manufacture of cheap cupboards, your first order is small, and you deliver 1 ton of the chipboard. Your customer is impressed and asks you to deliver 10 tons. You know you don't have the capabilities to meet the delivery deadline. DON'T just say "yes" and then figure it out later. Rather be honest and tell the customer that you have to do X, Y, and Z before you can fulfill an order that big. Honesty is appreciated, and I am sure that said customer will perhaps order another ton, but ask you to aim at 10 tons per month, six months from the date. At that point, you can do what needs to be done, in order to fulfill the customers' requirements. Don't forget to sign a supply contract first! (I will carry on repeating this one, it is very important).

Not Doing Proper Bookkeeping

Absolutely everything needs to be correctly recorded. In your first month, perhaps you have only a few transactions, and it is easy to record them. In month two there are a few more, but you put off doing your spreadsheet until the month after, as you are focusing on sales. By the time you get around to recording the transactions, your bank statement reflects items that you don't remember, and it takes you far too long to search for invoices and to pinpoint what charges are what. Don't let it get away from you! This is why physical files are important.

Keep every single slip and invoice and estimate and anything else that involves money coming in and out. You want to be able to do your own books for as long as possible before paying someone to do them. There will be cases where you need a bookkeeper from day one, but even then, you need to keep slips, invoices, etc., to give to your bookkeeper so that he or she stays on top of recording all transactions. There is nothing worse than "tax season" arriving and having to spend hours getting copies of invoices and trawling through months of bank statements to identify unrecorded transactions.

Not Coming Up With a Marketing Plan

As we all know, marketing is huge. If nobody knows about your product or service, then nobody is going to buy your product or use your service. Marketing differs depending on what your business does, but below is an adaptable outline of what a marketing plan should look like.

Your Business's Mission

Take a joinery and fitment company as an example: "*We aim to provide all-inclusive fitment solutions, from first measure to final installation.*" You can also use the mission or part of it as a tagline for your business, "*ABC joinery, from measure to perfection.*"

Define your Key Performance Indicators

Key Performance Indicators or KPI's are the metrics used to judge the who, how, and what of marketing. The most obvious example is online marketing, so tracking your social media likes, views and comments can give you an idea of what marketing content is receiving a positive response. In the joinery market, there will be expos and trade shows that you can target as part of your exposure campaign. Word of mouth is even a metric that can be defined.

For instance, get customers to fill out a short survey form and gather that information to hone in on what works for your target market.

Identify the Type of Person That Wants Your Product

One way to get this information is via your KPI's, but also via understanding what demographic likes your product. Perhaps you manufacture sportswear, and a major product is trendy lycra yoga pants for women. Your target market would likely be young, sporty women that are health and fashion-conscious.

Record Your Marketing Strategy

This can be in list or point form and may look something like this:

- Summer trade shows

- Advert in XYZ magazine

- Customer feedback forms

- Mailing list

- YouTube content campaign

- Blog

The above isn't specific to any one type of business, just a basis for how to form a strategy.

What Not to Focus On

You know what your target market is, so you can identify the demographic that you are not targeting. You don't want to waste your marketing budget on a demographic that has no need or use for your product.

Record Your Budget

It is vital to know how much money you have available and to what elements of marketing it is allocated. Be specific and remember that even if you have a limited budget, there are a whole lot of free marketing opportunities.

Identify Your Competition

You need to know who and/or what you are trying to out-market and out-sell. You can also learn from your competition. If you don't know anything about your competitors, they already have the edge over you.

Hiring the Wrong People

A formal interview is the most commonly used hiring method, but remember, prospective employees are going to tell you what they think you want to hear. We often misjudge people, thinking that we have found the right person for the job, only to discover that such isn't the case. If you think about it, someone who is unemployed needs to find a job to generate an income. That means that such a person will cast the net wide, and send his/her resume to as many companies as possible. Their objective may be to secure the first job that they can, to get an income, and then carry on applying for the job that they really want.

Do as many checks as you can before making a decision on staff. Very often, employers will choose employees based on an interview without getting hold of that person's references. It is generally accepted that a resume contains the contact details of former employers, so contacting them isn't difficult and should not be overlooked.

Over-Promising and Under-Delivering

Don't put yourself in a situation where you commit to a date and then cannot deliver on or before that date. Simply put, under-promise and over-deliver. Give yourself some breathing room to allow for unforeseeable delays. If you fail to meet a commitment, you will look very bad, and in those cases, word travels fast.

Failing to Understand the Demands of Business

When you go into a new venture, expect to work hard, expect early mornings and long days, expect stress, and never think it will be easy. If you are an employee, you have one job, but as an owner or shareholder, there is a lot to get done. When the clock ticks over to 5 p.m., that doesn't mean that you can go home. You have to do what needs to be done to drive your business toward success. If you are half-hearted about your business, it will never work.

Chapter Summary

Statistics show that a large portion of new businesses fails. The possible mistakes set out in this chapter are to make sure that your business is not among the adverse statistics. Not only do you have to have a plan, work hard, and be organized, but you also have to know when the time comes to hire people. When you can't get through all your work day to day, and your business starts to suffer, you require help, and it is out there. Be cautious, though.

Avoid the wrong investors and make sure you understand your capital requirements. Don't dive in too quickly, also don't hire too quickly. Make sure you know your target market, and your competitors. Include these things in your marketing plan, keep your books up to date, and be prepared to put in the hard yards. The contents of this chapter are as important, if not more important, than the administrative side of your S-Corp set-up, so please, I urge you to take them to heart.

Chapter 14

ACCOUNTING AND TAX FOR YOUR S-CORP

Accounting/bookkeeping are important, and tax forms are scary, but don't panic. Below is an explanation of both so you have an idea of what it all entails before you have that first meeting or interview with your prospective accounting and tax expert.

Your S-Corp will receive invoices and issue invoices. An invoice is basically a list of things sold or services given, with an amount payable for such things or services. It is important to use a numbering system or reference system so that you can easily locate invoices when required.

An invoice should contain the name of your S-Corp, or trading name, as well as your S-Corp's address and your customer's name and address. Furthermore, an invoice must have your S-Corps banking details and instructions on how to pay. A clear reference number must be printed onto the invoice, and in the payment instructions, you must request that the customer stipulates the reference number when making payment.

This makes it a lot easier to allocate payment receipts to specific payments and prevents the need to trawl through pages of bank statements to reconcile invoices. An invoice does not have to be complicated or have unnecessary information. The next paragraph is the rough wording of an invoice, but there are many ways to set out the information on a written document.

Invoice from: XYZ Corp, 123 First Avenue, Nutbush, on X date 2022, to ABC Housing, 456 Second Avenue, Nutbush. For: Plumbing services rendered on Y date 2022, in the amount of $500, due on or before Z date 2022. XYZ Corp's banking details are PayPal xxxxxx. When making payment, please use reference number 135-Ab, to allow us to allocate the payment.

Your S-Corp will also receive invoices that should have the above information; it really is just the layout that will change. After payment, then a receipt is raised as proof that the invoice has been paid.

Receipt of: $500 paid by ABC Housing, 456 Second Avenue, Nutbush, to XYZ Corp, 123 First Avenue, Nutbush, on X date 2022, for plumbing services rendered on Y date 2022, allocated under reference number 135-Ab.

How to Keep Accounting Records

The basic principles of bookkeeping are an accepted set of uniform rules in general, but depending on your entity and your choice of taxation, they will differ slightly. Financial statements will be scrutinized at your shareholder's meeting, if you have more than one shareholder. The information contained therein must be specific and as correct as possible. It is not uncommon that the S-Corps financial statements will need to be adjusted slightly.

Smaller things, such as recording the purchase of office fungibles as a petty cash expense when they were actually purchased with the company credit card, and similar transactions, occur frequently. As long as the money in and money out are correct on your balance sheet, the finer details can be corrected with no problem. Here are the basics that you need to do:

Collect and Capture

It sounds self-explanatory, but it is the DOING that is important. The "collect" means to collect any proof of transaction, i.e., sales invoices, copies of checks, and even slips for small day-to-day purchases. Absolutely everything! Avoid cash-in-hand transactions without any proof, but if you do, then record the transaction immediately.

My advice is to open files and file copies of everything. If your S-Corp is a grocery store, it is likely that every till will produce a print-out every day as part of the point-of-sale system. If you neglect to record the transactions and/or file them, even if your system generates the same, you will fall behind and create more work for yourself or your accountant/bookkeeper.

Your General Ledger

If I had a dollar every time I heard the term "general ledger," I would be a wealthy man. However, the common use of the term indicates that it is an accounting document that garners regular use. General ledgers use the double-entry system of accounting and are often kept quarterly, but I prefer to keep them monthly or even weekly if you are passing a significant amount of transactions. Here is a very simple example that will give you the basics of what a general ledger is. I am only going to include one expense (weekly rent) to keep it just to the fundamentals.

Note that week one and week two rent was paid on time. The rent for week three was not paid in week three, meaning that in week four your C-Corp paid "double rent" to leave a balance of zero. This is just an example; don't pay your rent late.

General Ledger of ABC Trading for the month of June 2022:

DATE	Details	Ref	Debit	Credit	Balance
1–7 June	Rent	JR-1	1000	1000	0
8–15 June	Rent	JR-2	1000	1000	0
16–22 June	Rent	JR-3	1000	0	1000
23–30 June	Rent	JR-4	1000	2000	0
Closing Bal					0

Financial Statements

Usually, financial statements are produced annually and reflect the profit or loss of your S-Corp. The concept is simple, assets-liabilities. There are some assets that do not seem like assets at first. The obvious ones are money in the bank, recorded as "cash," and the value of anything that your S-Corp owns, such as a company vehicle. Money owed to your S-Corp is an asset.

Even though it isn't in your account yet, it will be when it becomes due (and paid). If you pay anything in advance, for instance, utilities, the amount is also an asset because, technically, it is still your money. Finally, your stockholding is an asset. It belongs to your S-Corp until it is sold.

Liabilities are made up of anything that your S-Corp owes or will owe, in the case of a 30-day account, for example. This includes monies owed but not yet due as repayments on a start-up loan or other type of finance.

If you are confused at this point, you need a bookkeeper. Don't worry if you are confused. You don't have any formal training in accounting, so actually, you should be confused.

Close out Your Financials

Closing out your financials is a crucial step in the accounting process. At the end of each accounting period, typically at the end of a fiscal year, businesses perform a financial close to reconcile their accounts and prepare for the upcoming period. This involves systematically reviewing all financial transactions recorded during the period.

During the financial close, businesses ensure that all income and expense accounts are accurately recorded. This includes reviewing bank statements, invoices, receipts, and other financial documents to verify the accuracy of entries. Any discrepancies or errors are identified and corrected.

Once the reconciliation is complete, the accounts are 'closed,' meaning that their balances are transferred to the appropriate financial statement accounts. For example, revenue and expense accounts are closed into the income statement, while any dividends are closed to the retained earnings account on the balance sheet.

Closing out financials serves several purposes. It helps maintain the accuracy of financial records, provides a clear snapshot of the business's financial health at the end of the period, and ensures a smooth transition into the new accounting period. Starting the next period with a clean slate, or 'zeroing out,' facilitates accurate financial reporting and analysis.

This process is typically facilitated by accounting software, but regardless of the tools used, attention to detail and accuracy is paramount. The financial close is a fundamental practice for businesses seeking transparency, compliance, and a solid foundation for future financial decisions.

Tax Time

When you are done with all of the above, you can file your return on Form 1120-S, available on the IRS website. Before we get there, it is necessary to lay out the why(s) and what(s) of S-Corps.

Employee Taxation

The reason for the development of S-Corps and pass-through taxation was to take tax pressure off smaller corporations, and the IRS has successfully done so. Employees have to be looked after in terms of medical care or unemployment, amongst other financial considerations, which means that S-Corps have to pay the following employee-related taxes.

Medicare and Social Security Taxes

The IRS requires S-Corps to withhold and pay Medicare and Social Security Taxes. Your S-Corp is also, as per IRS regulations, obliged to add their contribution to their employee tax. The percentage rate can vary from time to time, but you are looking at approximately 15.3% of each employee's wages.

Federal Unemployment Tax

The IRS requires S-Corps to pay this tax for permanent employees. It is a contingency for unexpected circumstances in which a worker finds themselves unemployed, so they can claim compensation. The rate is about 6% of each employee's wages.

Excess Net Passive Investment Tax

S-Corps were not intended as entities with large amounts of passive income, and as a result, S-Corps with significant passive income receipts are subject to corporation tax. The ruling is that an S-Corp that earns passive income is not responsible for tax on the first 25% of gross receipts, but any gross receipts that exceed the 25% mark do pay corporate tax on the percentage exceeded.

Shareholder Taxation

Federal Income Tax

S-Corp shareholders logically pay tax on their share of earnings accredited to the S-Corp. The tax rates fall within a large range, between 10% and 37%, even if the amounts due have not yet been distributed. It makes sense in that the money is essentially "owed" by the S-Corp to its shareholders.

Net Investment Income Tax

This form of tax applies to high-income earning shareholders who are not employees of the S-Corp. The high-income earning category is $200,000 per annum. If you are a couple that files your returns as such together, the threshold is $250,000 per annum. Remember that the tax applies to anything above the threshold and is set at exactly 3.8%.

State Income Tax

The rates differ from state to state, but they are relatively low, so no need to put a huge focus on this in terms of structure.

State Franchise Tax

Most states impose franchise tax requirements, and like State Income Tax, the rates vary, but there is an extra consideration for Franchise Tax, being the S-Corps annual income.

State Sales Tax

Like the above two categories, tax is most often payable on sales and/or income from services rendered, and the rates also vary from state to state.

Excise Tax

This tax is imposed on goods that are locally manufactured.

Unemployment and Workers Compensation Insurance

Most states require this of S-Corp shareholders for the same reason that non-shareholder employees benefit from Federal Unemployment Tax in adverse or unforeseen employment situations.

Tax Optimization

There are ways in which businesses can be structured in order to make them as tax effective as possible. At the end of the day, we all want to pay as little as possible… legally.

W-2 Income

If you have more than one shareholder, and one or more of your shareholders receive an employment income, otherwise known as W-2, you can structure the salaries on your S-Corp, so that shareholders with W-2 income are paid less. The salary still has to be reasonable for what that shareholder does, but having an employment income outside of the S-Corp means that such shareholders will dedicate less time to the S-Corp, thus justifying a smaller salary. The specific reason and saving come in due to the fact that smaller salaries can be kept below the social security tax threshold.

Husband and Wife High-Income Earners, Plus Children on the Payroll

This exercise keeps either the husband or the wife under the social security and Medicare tax thresholds. Let's say that they both earn $120,000; the entire $240,000 attracts social security and Medicare tax. If the wife was paid $200,000 and the husband $40,000, the husband's income is below the threshold, and the total tax saving is $8,750. You can also get your children to work after hours or during holidays as a way to even out family income to minimize tax.

Gifts

This one is not advisable, as it blurs the lines slightly, but if there is someone that your company is supporting, amounts can be paid and labeled as gifts to make income distribution look as if it falls under tax brackets. It is not illegal, but it borders on it, so if you choose to do this, please be very careful.

Form 1120-S

Now that you know the types of tax, we can get to the dreaded tax form, 1120-S. Depending on the size of your S-Corp, some sections of the form will be irrelevant. Like with anything, if you have never done it, then you will not know how to do it. For this part of the running of your S-Corp, you absolutely need a specialist. When your S-Corp is still growing, you probably want to hire a tax expert as and when needed, but this form you have to get correct.

I will set out the basics below, split into sections. Note that the form does not refer specifically to parts, so I have divided the form into parts. Before I get there, I want to reiterate that you should not attempt this on your own unless you are formally trained or have experience in filing tax returns.

Part 1: Details

This part is easy; it requires all the information you already have at hand, like the name of S-Corp, EIN, address, date incorporated, number of shareholders, and other basic information.

Part 2: Income

I am not going to stipulate every single income line. The idea is to keep it simple and get the basics across.

This information is extracted from your accounting records and will look like this:

- Sales minus stock returns
- Cost of stock sold
- Gross profit/loss

- Net profit/loss

- Other income

- Total income

Part 3: Expenses

The same applies to focusing on the basics. This information also comes from your accounting records.

- Salaries

- Repairs to machinery

- Rent

- Interest

- Marketing

- Miscellaneous expenses

- Ordinary income/loss

Part 4: Tax and Payments

This is where complications come in, but the end result is your estimated tax, often referred to as a provisional tax. There are sections for passive income tax, as well as rebates, such as a returnable tax on fuel and tax penalties due to prior late filing. There is a section that requires an estimate of overpaid tax and an explanation of the calculations of each line item, depending on amounts and percentages.

Part 5: Other Information (Referred to as Schedule B on the Form)

This part starts with questions as to whether your S-Corp (other corporation) uses cash or accrual accounting, what the S-Corps primary business activity is, what the product is, and/or what service your S-Corp offers. It goes on to a list of questions about what I like to term "technicalities," such as whether a shareholder was classified as a disregarded entity.

This is a complicated language for asking if your entity is registered for pass-through tax. The other questions mostly deal with turnover thresholds, percentage ownership, and information applicable to trusts or entities other than an S-Corp. When completing this section, you absolutely have to know exactly what you are doing.

Part 6: Shareholders Pro rata Share Items (Referred to as Schedule K on the Form)

This section deals with what one could call ancillary income. It requires the stipulation of real estate portfolios, rental income, capital gains, and losses. Furthermore, there is a component that focuses on things like biofuel tax and stipulations irrelevant to an S-Corp, like foreign taxes.

Part 7: Balance Sheets per Book (Referred to as Schedule L on the Form)

This part is the assets and liabilities record. There are columns for asset values at the beginning and the end of the tax year, with areas to record depletable assets, shareholder loans, amortizable assets, and other categories whose names are hard to pronounce. Again, a large number of these sections are irrelevant to S-Corps.

Appoint an Expert

I am fully aware that I have been repeating this bit of advance, but I really do not want new business owners to attend to tax submissions on their own. I have stuck to the absolute basics, and from those, you can glean that the complicated parts have got to be addressed by an expert in the field.

Chapter Summary

Accounting/bookkeeping and tax returns are important from the point of view that if done correctly, the job of record-keeping becomes more effective. The term "collect and capture" describes the way in which you and your fellow shareholders and employees need to stay on top of the process. Every invoice, slip, check, and anything that forms proof of a transaction must be collected and captured into your accounting system AND must be filed physically.

The basis of accounting is maintaining a general ledger, the example of which is set out above. In addition, financial statements reflecting your S-Corps income or loss must be compiled and your financials closed out, from which point you can submit your tax returns.

Taxation is split into employee taxation and shareholder taxation, meaning non-shareholder employees, first off. Your S-Corp is subject to Medicare and Social Security Taxes, Federal Unemployment Tax, and Excess Net Passive Investment Tax. The latter is taxed highly as the S-Corp structure was not developed for largely passive income-earning businesses.

Shareholder taxation includes four types of state tax, i.e., Income, Franchise, Sales, and Excise Tax. The amounts differ from state to state, but in some states, not all four categories are taxed. The main taxation categories are Federal Income Tax and Net Investment Tax, which can be on the high side. Finally, the S-Corp is obliged to pay Unemployment and Workers Compensation Insurance, which caters to future situations of possible unemployment.

In terms of filing Form 1120-S, I broke up the sections, more for your information than the actual completion of the form. You want to get a tax expert, bookkeeper or accountant, or another expert to do this for you. If you attempt it yourself and make errors, you may cause your S-Corp to pay more tax than required. I would recommend sitting with your expert once he or she has completed the form, so they can explain it for your peace of mind.

SECTION II
A DEEPER DIVE INTO UNDERSTANDING TAX STRUCTURES - LLCS AND S-CORPS

Welcome to the next level of understanding tax structures: LLCs and S-Corps. In this new section, our goal is crystal clear: to equip small business owners with valuable insights and a collection of practical tips and tricks to help them maximize the tax advantages associated with both S-Corps and LLCs. Whether you're just starting out or looking to optimize your existing business structure, this section will provide you with the knowledge and tools you need to navigate the complexities of tax planning effectively. Let's dive in and explore how you can leverage these structures to your advantage!

CHAPTER 15
UNDERSTANDING TAX STRUCTURES - LLCS AND S-CORPS

Introduction to Tax/Business Structures

Have you ever thought about how your company's business structure could impact your entrepreneurial journey? Choosing between different business structures available is a strategic decision, with many tax implications. In this field, two types of business stand out, which are Limited Liability Companies (LLCs) and S-Corporations (S-Corps), and there are many reasons why.

While the tax implications of business structures may seem complex initially, having a grasp of them allows business owners to confidently navigate intricacies and make decisions tailored to their specific business requirements and objectives.

LLCs and S Corps provide businesses with benefits underscoring their importance. Understanding these two types of business structures empowers entrepreneurs to efficiently determine tax strategies potentially resulting in smaller tax burdens and increased savings.

Consequently small business owners can gain an understanding of business entities and their tax implications to determine optimal tax planning strategies for their ventures.

Brief Overview of Different Business Structures

Before going into details about LLCs and S-Corps, it is first important to explore the different business structures that are available for entrepreneurs in the United States when they decide to create their company.

The first business structure is the Sole Proprietorship. It is the simplest type of business structure, where only one person runs and manages the company. This person is personally liable, meaning she is responsible for all debts and liabilities of the company with her personal assets. Regarding taxation, there is no separate legal entity. As a result, all earnings and expenses are recorded on the owner's personal tax returns, which makes taxes pretty easy to handle for this type of business.

The second business structure is the Partnership. This is basically the plural version of the sole proprietorship. In a partnership, two or more people are owners of the company and manage the company. There is no separate legal entity, so owners are personally liable for the debts and liabilities of the business as well. And like a sole proprietorship, profits and losses are carried over to the partners' personal tax returns.

The third business structure is the C-Corporation (C-Corp). C-Corps are separate legal entities, which offer limited liability protection for their owners. It means that C-Corp owners are not liable for the debts and liabilities of the business. Moreover, in contrast to the different forms of partnerships, C-Corps are subject to double taxation: profits are taxed at the corporate level (due to the separate legal entity existing) and at the personal level, when owners receive dividends from the company.

The fourth business structure is the Limited Liability Company (LLC). LLCs combine the flexibility and tax benefits of a partnership with the limited liability protection of the C-corporation. In terms of tax consequences, LLCs are by default treated as partnerships, where business profits and losses are passed through to their owners' tax returns, which allows them to avoid double taxation (there is no taxation at the corporate level).

Finally, the fifth business structure is the S-Corporation (S-Corp). S-Corp is a specific type of corporation because it is a pass-through taxation company. Corporate profits and losses pass through their shareholders tax returns, just like partnerships and LLCs, which allow them to avoid double taxation. In this business structure, shareholders can also benefit from the limited liability protection.

Focusing on LLCs and S-Corps

Let's dive into LLCs and S-Corps, examining their key features and how they differ from other business structures:

LLCs

To establish an LLC, the owner(s) must register the company by submitting articles of organization within the state of the incorporation and drafting an operating agreement that describes the structure and functioning of the company.

In terms of liability, LLCs offer their members limited liability protection, like Corporations, allowing members to separate personal assets from the liabilities and debts of the firm.

In terms of taxation, LLCs provide lots of flexibility. Members can choose to be taxed as a corporation (either C-corp or S-corp), or as a disregarded entity (like a sole proprietorship or partnership). However, by default, LLCs are considered pass-through businesses (unless you opt for another way), which means that business income and losses are passed through the owners' personal taxes. This simplifies taxation and avoids double taxation.

S-Corporations

To establish a S-Corp, you need to be eligible. To be eligible, you must fulfill specific requirements, such as having only one class of stock, being domestic, and having no more than 100 shareholders.

In terms of liability, S-Corp shareholders enjoy limited liability protection, which isolates personal assets from company debts and liabilities, like C-corporations and LLCs.

In terms of taxation, S-Corps are subject to pass-through taxation, like LLCs. It means that corporate profits and losses are recorded on the personal tax returns of the owners. However, S-Corps are subject to unique IRS laws and regulations, such as the regulations regarding the shareholders' salary. Shareholders who actively participate in the business must receive a 'reasonable remuneration', subject to payroll taxes, which prevents potential tax evasion and ensures compliance with IRS laws. However, if shareholders structure their compensation well, S-Corps allow them to save a lot of self-employment taxes, in comparison to other business structures.

Significance of Selecting the Right Structure for Tax Optimization

It is important to choose the right business structure because it heavily influences the firm's financial performance. There are several reasons why the right business structure can make a difference:

The first reason is that it may increase the company's tax efficiency. The tax burden required by the company is determined by the type of structure, which is why it is important to pick the right one so that it is as efficient as possible. If business owners do this successfully, it can help them maximize their profits and save significantly on tax. For instance, pass-through businesses such as LLCs and S-Corps allow corporate revenue to "pass-through" to owners' tax returns, which can lead to these owners paying less in taxes.

The second reason is personal liability. The right structure also determines the level of personal liability available to a firm's owners. This refers to liability protection and states that if a business fails, owners' personal assets cannot be used to pay the firm's debts and obligations. The level of such protection is different across corporate structures. In LLCs and corporations, owners benefit from a particularly high degree of liability protection since any corporate debts and obligations can be dealt with in the corporation alone. This applies unless the corporation is found guilty of fraudulent activity. If this is done properly, owners' personal assets are safe from the corporation's bankruptcy.

The third reason why it is important to choose the right structure for your business is the degree of flexibility that a company offers. This is variable depending on the type of company in question, for instance,

LLCs offer a very flexible management style compared to corporations, where shareholders need to respect administrative obligations that can be less flexible than in LLCs. This is the main reason why companies with multiple owners or owners who want to make something in the short term tend to prefer this type of business.

The fourth reason is about the requirement to remain compliant. All business entities have certain requirements related to the operation process, such as the process of registration, management, or even tax preparation and filing to government entities. Entrepreneurs shall respect all of these requirements otherwise they might face a penalty from the government or be dragged into a legal conflict. Therefore, when owners evaluate which business structure is most suitable for their company, they must also evaluate their capability to follow the requirements as well.

The fifth reason is related to the long term business goals and objectives. Some business structures facilitate owners more easily to pursue their goals and objectives long-term, while some do not. That is why the entrepreneurs must look at different elements, such as an exit plan, how their business can be passed on to the next generation, or the scalability of their business entities. For example, corporations may provide more options to issue shares or get funding from the outside world, but LLCs offer more freedom to distribute the profits and the ownership.

Overall, entrepreneurs need to pay very close attention to the selection of business structure. By understanding the difference between each entity, such as the limitation of liability, compliance with government process, whether their company meets the eligibility requirements, how flexible is their management and ownership structure, as well as their long-term business plans and goals, the business owners will take the informed decision in this important step.

Comparative Analysis of Tax Benefits and Breakdown of Tax Advantages Associated with LLCs and S-Corps

Owners should evaluate the tax benefits provided by the LLCs and S-Corps before selecting the right business structure for their business. Let's break down the tax benefits of each of these two structures and compare them:

Tax Benefits of LLCs	Tax Benefits of S-Corps
Pass-Through Taxation: LLCs offer pass-through taxation, which means that business revenues and losses are immediately reflected on the owners' personal tax returns. This avoids double taxes and ensures profits are taxed exclusively at the individual level.	**Pass-Through Taxation:** S-Corps also use pass-through taxes, which ensures that corporate revenue and losses pass through to shareholders' personal tax returns and eliminates double taxation.

Tax Treatment Flexibility: LLC owners have the option to select their tax treatment. By default, LLCs are treated as disregarded companies or partnerships, but owners can choose to be taxed as S-Corps or C-Corps based on their optimization goals.	**Self-Employment Tax Reduction**: S-Corp shareholders can minimize their self-employment tax liability. They can organize their income by taking fair compensation and distributing remaining profits or earnings as dividends, which are not subject to self-employment taxes.
Deduction of Business Expenses: LLC owners can deduct business expenses including operating costs, payroll, and office supplies from their taxable income, lowering their total tax obligation.	**Tax Planning Flexibility**: S-Corps also provides flexibility in tax planning. Shareholders can manage compensation and distributions of dividends to reduce tax liability while increasing after-tax earnings.
Limited Liability Protection: LLCs provide limited liability protection to members, shielding personal assets from business debts and legal liabilities.	**Fringe Benefits**: S-Corps can provide employees and shareholders with fringe benefits like health insurance and retirement plans. These benefits are deductible as

	business expenses, which reduces taxable income.

Comparative Analysis

To better understand the tax benefits of LLCs and S-Corps, let us compare the two side by side in a simpler and straightforward manner:

Tax Benefit	LLCs	S-Corps
Pass-Through Taxation	Yes	Yes
Flexibility in Tax Treatment	Yes	Limited to S-Corp Election
Avoidance of Self-Employment Taxes	N/A	Yes
Deduction of Business Expenses	Yes	Yes
Limited Liability Protection	Yes	Yes

Tax Planning Opportunities	Moderate	Significant
Fringe Benefits	Yes	Yes

LLCs and S-Corps come with different tax benefits. LLCs provide both tax flexibility and protection of limited liability, while S-Corps provide business owners with opportunities for tax planning and the chance to save on substantial self-employment taxes. A business entity's (and its owners') individual goals and needs are ultimately what would determine if an LLC or an S-Corp is a better fit for them.

Explanation of How Each Structure Offers Unique Opportunities for Small Business Owners

Now, let's see what each structure brings to the table from the entrepreneur's perspective:

Business Structure	Unique Opportunities
Sole Proprietorship	Sole proprietorships are the simplest business entity, with minimal paperwork and regulatory requirements.

	Owners are also in full control of their businesses, giving them the ability to make decisions quickly and adapt easily.
	With sole owners, these company expenses could be deducted on the owner's personal tax return, thus reducing taxable income.
Partnership	Partnerships enable owners to share responsibilities and resources, leveraging the knowledge and expertise of numerous individuals.
	Pass-through taxes, where the report of profits and losses is made on the personal taxes of their partners, which may lower tax burden.
	Partnerships can be structured to allow different degrees of managerial authority, allowing partners to have different degrees of responsibilities and contributions.
	C-Corporations offer shareholders limited liability protection, separating personal assets from business debts and liabilities.

Corporation (C-Corp)	To raise money and expand, enterprises can issue stocks to investors.
	Corporate tax rates might be lower than individual tax rates for certain income levels.
Limited Liability Company (LLC)	LLCs protect members' personal assets from business debts and legal liabilities.
	LLCs allow members to pass-through revenue and losses to their personal tax returns, eliminating the liability of being double-taxed.
	LLCs allow for more flexibility in management structure, profit-sharing and ownership structures.
S-Corporation (S-Corp)	S-Corps are also subject to pass-through taxation, which may reduce the total tax burden, largely by avoiding double taxation.
	Like an LLC owner, an S-Corp owner can take home income as salary and dividends, minimizing payroll taxes and maximizing tax savings.

	S-Corps are not available to all companies and must pass certain qualification restrictions, such as a limit on the number of shareholders and the particular forms of ownership permitted.

You can see from the table that each kind of business structure exists for owners ,and it has many benefits, such as management that could be more flexible, personal property that could be protected, and tax that can be simplified.

Choosing Between LLCs and S-Corps

Factors Influencing the Decision-Making Process

When deciding whether to create a Limited Liability Company (LLC) or an S-Corporation (S-Corp), entrepreneurs must evaluate a variety of factors to identify the best structure for their company needs. Below, we'll look at the key factors that would influence the business owner's decision, as well as the benefits and disadvantages of each structure.

Factors	LLCs	S-Corps
Liability Protection	Provides limited liability protection by separating owners' personal assets from corporate liabilities, debts and legal responsibilities. Members are not personally liable for the company's obligations.	Similar to LLCs, shareholders benefit from limited liability protection, protecting personal assets from business liabilities. Shareholders' personal assets are generally not at risk for business liabilities, debts or lawsuits.
Taxation	The default taxation structure is as a pass-through organization, which means that business income and losses are shown on the owners' personal tax returns. This often leads to simpler tax reporting and avoiding double taxation.	Also taxed as a pass-through entity, with business profits and losses reported on shareholders' personal tax returns. Like LLCs, S-Corps avoid double taxation, which can result in tax savings for shareholders.

Ownership and Management	Provides flexibility in ownership and management of the company. Members have the freedom to distribute profits and losses in proportions they consider appropriate, allowing for a tailored partnership arrangement. Management can be structured as member-managed or manager-managed, allowing for a greater flexibility in the decision-making process.	Limited to 100 shareholders, all of them must be US citizens or US residents. Ownership transferability may be limited, since S-Corps cannot issue multiple classes of stock. Management is typically structured with a board of directors overseeing day-to-day operations (management and structure not as flexible as LLCs).
Formalities and Compliance	Generally requires fewer formalities and compliance obligations compared to corporations: Minimal annual reporting obligations and minimal regulatory requirements, which results in a lower	Subject to higher compliance obligations, such as having annual shareholder meetings and keeping business documents. Compliance with the qualifying requirements is required to preserve S-Corp status, which may require

	administrative burden and cost.	additional administrative work.
Tax Planning and Optimizatio n	Offers flexibility in tax planning and tax optimization, allowing owners to choose the most favorable tax treatment for their company. Owners can choose to be taxed as a disregarded entity (like a sole proprietorship or partnership) or as a corporation (either C-Corp or S-Corp).	S-Corps provide tax advantages, including pass-through taxation, which may reduce shareholders' overall tax burden. However, certain constraints do apply, such as the need for stockholders to be paid appropriate remuneration, subject to payroll taxes.

Eligibility and Restrictions	Generally open to a wide range of businesses and industries, with fewer eligibility restrictions compared to S-Corps.	Subject to specific eligibility criteria set by the IRS, including having no more than 100 shareholders, being domestic, and having only one class of stock. Some individuals and entities, such as partnerships, corporations, and non-resident aliens, are ineligible for S-Corp status.

Practical Insights on Selecting the Most Suitable Tax Structure Based on Business Goals and Financial Considerations

Choosing the proper business structure for your company calls for first to decide special elements, including your business goals, financial goals, and operational needs. Here are some practical tips that will help you make this choice:

Start by identifying your short-term and long-term period business goals. Are you seeking to reduce tax burden, attract investors, or simplify business operations? Understanding your business objectives will help you prioritize elements like tax burden, flexibility in control and operations, administrative burden, or scalability whilst selecting a business structure.

Then, apprehend the tax implications of each business structure, which includes income tax, self-employment tax, and payroll taxes. For instance, LLCs and S-Corps each offer pass-through taxation, wherein company earnings are taxed on the owner's tax return. Which once in a while causes a lower tax burden in comparison to C-Corporations.

Next, determine the degree of liability protection you need for the members of the company. Corporations and LLCs provide limited liability protection, isolating personal assets from corporate debts, which, as said before, may be very important whilst things go down in the company. Partnerships, on the contrary, do not offer this protection.

Then, determine the management structure you prefer. Corporations have a much less flexible structure with lots of administrative responsibilities. It could probably lead to a longer decision-making process. On the other hand, LLCs offer greater flexibility in management, allocation of ownership, income-sharing arrangements and succession planning.

Next, understand the obligations of every business structure to stay compliant. Consider your ability to fulfill those necessities and make sure that you can continue to be legally compliant to prevent any penalties.

Finally, remember that your business wishes and desires can also change over time. Review your business structure often to confirm it is still in line with your company goals, and make required modifications if required. Keep updated on tax policies, and seek professional guidance to determine and implement the proper tax strategies.

By knowing your business needs, financial objectives, and operational goals, you may be able to choose the right business structure for your business, ensuring its success.

CHAPTER 16

ADVANCED TAX OPTIMIZATION STRATEGIES FOR S-CORPS

Deep Dive into S-Corp Tax Optimization

It is important for business owners to understand how tax strategies connected with S-Corps work, as it can drastically lower the amount of tax they pay and increase their profitability. S-Corps offer several characteristics and features that can be very useful to members. The upcoming chapter will look at its tax regime vis-à-vis its members in order to identify the strategies to implement.

In-depth Exploration of Advanced Tax Optimization Strategies Specific to S-Corps

There is a lot of room for small business owners to lower the tax burden within S-Corps, by taking advantage of advanced tax optimization strategies. In general, other corporations do not offer the same kind of planning opportunities as S-Corps.

One such strategy commonly used within an optimized S-corp taxation system is the careful management of shareholder compensation and distribution. The use of the right salaries and dividends by shareholders may reduce the business' tax obligations while maximizing earnings after tax. By doing this, S-Corps are able to maximize tax-efficient dividends while avoiding self-employment taxes.

Moreover, S-Corps can postpone revenue for later accounting periods by carefully scheduling distributions. These companies will be able to postpone paying taxes into several years by selecting exactly when to distribute earnings to shareholders. This may preserve liquidity and support future plans or projects for business growth. This strategy is especially helpful when distributions coincide with advantageous market circumstances, or when it is anticipated that future tax rates would likely decline.

Another important part of the S-Corp tax optimization strategy is the use of fringe benefits. S-Corps can offer a wide range of fringe benefits, such as retirement plans like 401(k) or SEP-IRA and health insurance, to both shareholders and employees. In addition to improving employee satisfaction and retention, this is a great way to significantly save in taxes. Through the deduction of fringe benefits as business expenses, S-Corps can lower their taxable income, while giving shareholders valuable advantages.

S-Corps can also use entity-level deductions to optimize their tax situation even further. S-Corps can reduce their total tax burden by strategically deducting business expenses at the entity level hence reducing taxable income. This strategy requires a thorough evaluation of permitted deductions of business expenses to remain compliant with tax regulations and guidelines.

In conclusion, exploring S-Corps tax optimization strategies provides many chances for small business owners to optimize their profitability.S-Corps can carefully choose the shareholder compensation and the time of their distribution, use fringe benefits and deduct business expenses at a corporate level to ultimately benefit the company's financial success.

Explanation of How S-Corps Can Be Leveraged For Maximum Tax Benefits

S-Corporations (S-Corps) enable small business owners to maximize their tax benefits in different ways. Here's a more detailed explanation on how S-Corps can be used to lower tax burden and increase business profits:

a. **Pass-Through Taxation**: One of the main benefits of S-Corps is pass-through taxation. Unlike C-Corps, where revenues are taxed both at a corporate and an individual level, S-Corps allow profits and losses to pass through to shareholders' personal tax returns. This means that the company itself does not pay any federal income taxes. Instead, shareholders report their pro rata share of income or loss incurred by the S-Corps on their tax returns, thus avoiding double taxation.

b. **Dividends vs. Salaries:** Compared to partners or single proprietors, S-Corp shareholders can lower the taxes related to their self-employment. Usually, self-employed persons must pay self-employment taxes on all business income. In S-Corps, shareholders can receive their full compensation in two parts: a part as a salary, and a part as dividends. Salaries are subject to employment taxes, but dividends are not, which allows shareholders to reduce the taxes they have to pay.

c. **Strategic Allocation:** S-Corps give shareholders freedom and flexibility in tax planning so that they can strategically allocate and manage their revenue. Shareholders can modify the amount of compensation they wish to receive, and the time they receive it. Through close collaboration with Tax experts, S-Corps shareholders can create strategized tax plans to timely allocate compensation and thus reduce the amount of taxes to pay.

d. **Fringe Benefits:** S-Corps can further enhance tax efficiency using fringe benefits. Retirement programs and health insurance premiums, in addition to other employee perks, are examples of fringe benefits. As opposed to direct compensation, they are deductible from revenue as business expenses. This reduces the taxable income of the company, allowing owners to significantly lower the amount of taxes they must pay, while keeping the employees satisfied.

e. **Estate Planning Options:** S-Corps provide shareholders and their heir with estate planning options that can result in considerable tax savings. By using strategic estate planning, including gifting shares, buy-sell agreements, trusts, estate freeze, family-limited partnerships (FLPs) and charitable giving, S-Corps shareholders can reduce estate taxes and make it easier for future generations to acquire the company.

Case Studies to Illustrate Successful Tax Optimization

Understanding small business owners need to understand tax strategies to increase their revenue while decreasing tax obligations. While theoretical principles are helpful, real-world scenarios and case studies provide concrete examples into how tax planning strategies work. In this section, we will analyze case studies and examples in order to demonstrate how S-Corps can benefit from tax benefits.

Scenario 1: Business Expenses

Like many other business structures, business owners of S-Corps can reduce their tax burden by deducting expenses related to the operation of the business. Some concrete examples include business-related travel expenses and office supplies. Business-related travel expenses are deductible, including transportation costs, meals, accommodations, or any other expenses linked to the travel. The deduction is not always to meet a client, it could also be to attend conferences, or even to explore new markets in a new country. Deducting these expenses can significantly reduce the taxable income, which is why it is crucial to document every business-related travel you undertake. On the other hand, office supplies may include computer equipment, software expenses, printer ink, and more. If these expenses directly contribute to the operation of the business, they are either deductible in full or can be depreciated over time depending on their nature. It is thus crucial here also to keep accurate records and receipts of your office supplies purchase.

Scenario 2: Home Office

If you are working from home, you may be eligible to deduct the percentage of your home that you use exclusively and repeatedly for running your business. Let's take an example. Imagine your house is

1,000 sq, and you use an office located in your house exclusively and repeatedly for running your company. This office is 200 sq representing 20% of the overall square footage. In that case, the IRS allows you to deduct 20% of your rent as a home-office expense. If the rent for the house is $2,000, you could thus deduct $400 (20% of the overall rent) as a home-office expense. But it does not end here. You are also eligible to deduct part of the utilities, part of the home insurance, part of the business-related expenses, and more. In that case, you can deduct 20% of each of these expenses since it is directly linked to the operation of your business from home.

Scenario 3: Salary vs. Dividends

Many single-member S-Corps owners apply the 60/40 rule. Under this rule, 60% of the business income goes to salary, and the remaining 40% would be considered as a distribution. This strategy allows owners to only pay personal income taxes on the salary amount (60%) rather than being taxed on the total business income, which can save a lot on taxes.

The IRS requires S-Corps to pay themselves a salary - the amount can be determined by the owner, as long as it meets the criterion to be a "reasonable compensation" (which would depend on the industry or marketplace). For example, a social media manager could receive up to $120,000 per year in a competitive marketplace. If this person forms a S-Corp, she would be able to pay herself a "reasonable compensation" as a salary (around $80,000 for instance) and treat the remaining $40,000 as a distribution from the S-Corp. But, according to the IRS requirements, she would not be able to consider only $12,000 as a salary.

Scenario 4: Tax Credits

S-Corps can qualify for different tax credits, which can further reduce the business's tax liability. Some concrete examples of tax credits would be: (1) R&D tax credits (Research and Development Tax Credits); (2) The Plug-In Electric Vehicle Credit; (3) The Alternative Motor Vehicle Credit; (4) The New Markets Credit; (5) The Retirement Plan Startup Costs Tax Credit; among others. It is highly advised to consult a tax expert to identify which tax credits you could use and further save on taxes.

Insights into How Businesses Have Benefited from S-Corp Tax Advantages

Understanding the field of tax strategies is essential for companies that are looking to maximize their profits. S-Corp is a type of structure that stands out in terms of tax optimization opportunities. In this paragraph, we will talk about how companies can use unique features and advantages that S-Corps provide in order to lower the tax burden.

a. **Transfer of Ownership:** Unlike other business structures, such as C-Corps, owners of S-Corps can freely transfer their interests without triggering significant tax consequences. It could be very beneficial for owners looking to plan for the future, or if they are not planning to stay long in the company. They could easily pass ownership to their family members, bringing in new partners, or even selling shares to investors.

b. **Cash method of accounting:** There are two primary methods that businesses use to record financial transactions and report them to the IRS: the cash method of accounting and the accrual method of accounting. Under the cash method, income and expenses are recorded when they are received or paid out, respectively. Under the accrual method, income and expenses are recorded when they are earned, regardless of when cash is actually received. Unlike C-corps, which required most of the time to use the accrual method of accounting, S-Corps have more flexibility. Unless they have inventory, S-Corps are not required to use the accrual method. If an S-Corps does not have inventory, it can use the cash method, which simplifies the record-keeping and provides a clearer picture of cash flow.

c. **Credibility:** Rather than operating as a sole proprietorship or a partnership, operating under an S-Corp can help the new business build credibility with investors, customers, employees, and even partners. They see this structure as a more formal commitment made by shareholders to their business.

d. **Protection of Assets:** S-Corps are separate legal entities from their shareholders, allowing shareholders to benefit from limited liability protection. It means that shareholders are not personally responsible for the debts and liabilities of the business and that business creditors cannot pursue the personal assets of any shareholders, such as the money in their personal bank accounts, their house, their mortgage, or their items of furniture, to pay the business debts and be reimbursed.

S-Corps gives companies multiple ways to maximize tax advantages, allowing companies to pay less taxes and grow faster. Effective use of these strategies can make a big difference in the long run, protecting their shareholders from personal liability, while contributing to the business's long-term development.

Common Mistakes to Avoid

Identification and Discussion of Pitfalls that Small Business Owners May Encounter

Small business owners may find it difficult to understand tax optimization strategies, especially if they are not familiar with the different procedures to implement. To optimize tax benefits from the S-Corp structure, it is also important to recognize the pitfalls that exist in order to avoid them. Let's explain some of the most recurrent errors we can see under the S-Corp:

a. **Misclassification of Shareholder Compensation:** A frequent mistake made by small business owners is to incorrectly categorize the compensation of the shareholders. As we explained before, all S-Corp shareholders who actively participate in the operation of the business must receive a "reasonable salary", which can vary depending on the industry and the local market. Underpaying shareholder-employees can result in important fines from the IRS. As a result, it is highly advised to consult a tax expert, who would be able to determine the right remuneration for these shareholders.

b. **Improper Documentation of Business Expenses:** Another common mistake is not properly documenting business expenses. To make proper deductions from the taxable income, owners must keep a precise record of all business expenses that have been made. Failing to do that could lead to audit risks, and would lead to potential significant fines from the IRS. It is thus recommended that business owners use a reliable accounting system, or work closely with an accountant or CPA, to efficiently monitor spending so that you can ensure your full compliance with the IRS regulations.

c. **Inadequate Understanding of Tax Regulations:** As we said before, small business owners must understand tax regulations. A lack of knowledge can result in compliance problems, and in paying too much taxes. To maintain compliance with regulations, small business owners must make an effort to stay updated and educated about it. If this is a complicated task, you can always consult with tax experts, who will be able to guide you through the new regulations.

d. **Failure to Implement Tax Planning Strategies:** Many small company owners miss out on potential tax savings because they fail to successfully apply the strategies we have previously detailed. There are numerous tax opportunities for tax planning, such as retirement plans, salary allocation, fringe benefits, and specific credits that owners can implement to their S-Corp. To maximize these advantages, it is recommended to consult with tax experts, who can develop a customized tax plan for your company, fully tailored to your industry and business activity.

e. **Ignoring State-Specific Tax Considerations:** Many small business owners also ignore state-specific tax laws and regulations, thinking only about federal tax laws. Tax rules and regulations, including income tax rates, franchise taxes, and sales tax obligations vary from state to state, which could affect your S-Corp. To take advantage of state-specific tax laws, owners should seek advice from tax specialists.

f. **Lack of Regular Tax Reviews and Updates**: Lastly, it is very frequent for small business owners to not stay updated on changes in tax regulations. Even minor revisions can have a significant impact on their tax obligations. To overcome this, we recommend conducting frequent tax audits with a tax specialist. These audits should evaluate and assess the owner's tax situation and identify the areas for improvement based on the changes in regulations, allowing them to continuously improve their tax strategy.

Practical Tips on How to Steer Clear of Common Errors in S-Corp Tax Optimization

S-Corp tax regulations are not easy, and understanding them takes time and requires close attention to detail. As we already explained the common errors that owners make under S-Corp, let's now take a look at different tips S-Corp shareholders should implement, which summarize everything we have discussed in this chapter.

1. **Maintain accurate financial records:** To make sure S-Corp shareholders are in conformity with tax laws, they should maintain thorough records of their revenue and their business expenses. It would prevent errors and inconsistencies during tax preparations, and would thus lower the risk of audits and fines by the IRS.

2. **Keep personal and business expenses separate:** To conform with tax regulations, expenses made for business or personal purposes must remain separate. Combining both types of expenses would create complexity, and ambiguity, and can lead to not being compliant with IRS regulations. As a result, owners should avoid using company cash for personal expenses and should have two separate bank account.

3. **Strategically allocate shareholder compensation:** As we explained before, the classification of S-Corp shareholders' compensation plays a crucial role in the tax consequences. To lower the self-employment taxes you would have to pay, pay yourself a "reasonable salary" and pay the remaining

compensation as dividends. To calculate the right amount that should be paid as salary, take into account industry and market standards, and consult a tax expert.

4. **Stay compliant with tax regulations:** S-Corp owners are responsible for keeping an eye on their tax strategies to make sure laws are being respected. To avoid going over what is acceptable, business owners should periodically review and understand the basis and modify their habits if necessary. It is often advised to consult with tax professionals for that.

5. **Stay updated with tax regulations:** Linked to the precedent tip, being aware of any changes in tax regulations is crucial. Tax law changes and it often has a consequence on the strategies owners should implement. To be informed about modifications, owners should read tax publications regularly, speak with tax experts, or even participate in seminars and workshops.

6. **Seek professional guidance:** As a last tip, we advise consulting with tax specialists, which is one of the best ways to avoid frequent mistakes in taxes. Because tax rules and regulations are complicated, and this is often not the owners' specialty, it can be difficult to navigate them without professional help. Owners should collaborate with tax experts who focus on S-Corp taxes to create a tailored tax plan suited to their requirements, allowing them to save a lot on taxes and invest in the long-term development of their company.

With careful planning, close attention to detail, and expert advice, mistakes can be avoided. Businesses can avoid common pitfalls by keeping accurate records, keeping separate records for personal and business expenses, making sure to properly allocate shareholder compensation, staying updated with tax regulations, and finally seeking professional advice. Business owners must understand that these tips would significantly lower their tax burden and position themselves for long-term profitability.

CHAPTER 17
PRACTICAL TIPS AND TRICKS FOR LLC TAX OPTIMIZATION

Key Considerations for LLC Tax Optimization

Business owners must know the unique tax benefits of Limited Liability Companies (LLCs) to maximize tax efficiency. LLCs are advantageous in several ways, such as the pass-through treatment of taxes, protection against personal assets, and flexibility in governance and taxation. In this chapter, we will take a look at the different strategies to implement to maximize these advantages linked to the LLC's tax treatment.

Exploration of Fundamental Strategies for Optimizing Taxes within an LLC

Understanding the unique tax benefits that Limited Liability Companies (LLCs) offer is a necessary step when selecting the best business structure for a company. LLCs are known to offer many tax advantages, such as pass-through taxation, limited liability protection for their owners, and a flexible tax treatment. The pass-through taxation allows owners to avoid double taxation since there is no taxation at the corporate level: the profits and losses of companies pass through to the stakeholders' personal tax returns.

Selection of the Tax Treatment

LLCs with one member are usually taxed as partnership by default, which means that the revenue goes through to the owner's personal tax return. However, for multi-member LLCs, owners have the option to be taxed as a corporation (either S-Corp or C-Corp). Therefore, it is important for LLC owners to select the best tax treatment for LLC, even after selecting that an LLC is the best business structure. Each tax treatment has pros and cons, and the decision will ultimately depend on the business goals and its activities.

Deductions and Credits

Another essential optimization strategy is to keep a thorough record of all business expenses. Keeping thorough financial records is essential for tracking spending, filing taxes, and making deductions. To lower their taxable income, LLC owners can take advantage of the credits and deductions that are permitted by regulations. Business expenses deductible by LLCs include rent, utilities, salaries, equipment, supplies, and services from professionals. Some tax incentives may help reduce the overall tax burden, such as the Small Business Health Care Tax Credit or the Work Opportunity Tax Credit.

Tax Strategy Implementation

Proper optimization of LLC taxes requires careful tax planning. LLC owners can strategically plan transactions to reduce their tax burden. Deferring revenue, increasing expenses, and making retirement plans are a few examples of strategies that can help LLCs minimize their tax obligations.

Changes in Tax Laws

Owners of LLCs should always keep up with any changes to tax laws and regulations that can have an impact on their company. Staying updated will allow owners to modify their strategy efficiently and capitalize on new available tax incentives or tax benefit opportunities.

In the end, LLC stakeholders have the opportunity to reduce their taxes and increase their profits by using specific strategies, such as maintaining meticulous records, taking advantage of eligible credits and deductions, implementing a tax strategy, and staying updated with changes.

Here's a checklist to guide you through the process:

Key Considerations for LLC Tax Optimization	Completed
Tax Classification	[ ]
Record-Keeping	[ ]

Deductions and Credits	[ ]
Tax Planning	[ ]
Stay Informed	[ ]

Highlighting the Unique Aspects of Tax Planning for LLCs

Limited Liability Companies (LLCs) are different from other business structures such as S-Corporations in that they provide a unique set of advantages and benefits in tax planning. It is thus crucial that small business owners understand these particular characteristics, or unique aspects, if they want to maximize their tax strategies.

The first unique aspect is the flexibility of tax treatment that LLCs offer.

LLCs are taxed as pass-through organizations by default, like partnerships or sole proprietorships. This prevents double taxation at the corporate and individual levels since there is no taxation at the corporate level. Business gains and losses pass through to the stakeholders' tax returns. It can stream the tax filing process and, if the business has losses, can make stakeholders benefit from these losses since it would diminish their overall personal tax burden.

However, when we say that LLCs are flexible in terms of tax treatment, this is because stakeholders have the choice to opt to be taxed as a corporation (either S-Corp or C-Corp). This selection can sometimes be advantageous, such as when stakeholders want to retain earnings within the company for future plans or projects, to benefit from the S-

Corps tax opportunities that we explained in the previous chapter, or even for benefitting from the C-Corporation flat tax rate, which can be tax-efficient in some case.

The second unique aspect is the flexibility in profit distribution among members.

LLCs are allowed to distribute earnings among their members more freely than S-Corps, which are required to distribute profits proportionally to their ownership in the company. In LLCs, this is possible to distribute, for instance, 90% of the earnings to a member that has 10% of ownership in the company. In that case, members draft a tailored operating agreement, and it is advised to be accompanied by a lawyer to prepare it, as it becomes a crucial agreement for the members. The operating agreement would define the way of functioning of the company but also define how earnings will be distributed among members. Members can create a unique profit-sharing plan that would take other criteria, such as capital contributions, the involvement of the company, and more. LLC members can thus customize profit allocation to meet their unique financial situation and corporate goals.

The third unique aspect is the very few administrative obligations.

Compared to corporations (either S-Corps or C-Corps), LLCs have fewer administrative obligations. LLCs are not required to follow the same processes. For instance, LLCs are not required to keep up with corporate records or hold several annual meetings. This results in less administrative work, a higher chance to stay compliant with regulations, and potential cost savings.

The fourth aspect is the limited liability protection for the members.

To be honest, this aspect is not entirely unique as corporations offer the same privilege to their members. However, it is an important aspect that we had to discuss. The limited liability protection granted to members allows them to protect their personal assets and separate them from business assets. As a result, in the event of lawsuits or bankruptcy, credits cannot seek repayment or reimbursement from the members' personal assets.

LLCs differ from other business structures in several ways, and the ability to choose their tax treatment is one of the most distinctive characteristics. LLCs give small business owners a flexible structure, with tailored profit distribution agreements, few administrative needs, flexible tax treatments, and flexibility in management.

Implementation of LLC Tax Saving Techniques

Practical Tips and Tricks for Small Business Owners to Implement Tax-saving Strategies

Now that you are well aware of the different aspects of LLCs, it is important to develop the strategies and tips that small business owners can implement to their LLCs to implement tax-saving strategies.

First Tip: Deduct Many Business Expenses

As an LLC, most expenses related to the operation of the business are tax-deductible. It means that they can be deducted from the taxable gross income. This results in paying less taxes, so it is advisable to make as many business-related expenses as possible to reduce the tax burden. The IRS regulations allow owners to deduct various operational costs, including start-up costs, such as legal fees, research fees, permits fees, travel expenses, materials, and equipment. It is also allowed to deduct property or rent expenses, self-employment taxes, business meals and entertainment expenses, phone and internet fees, office supplies, and other expenses up to a certain extent.

It is highly advised to keep track of all business expenses and stay organized to make it easier when taxes are due. Well-maintained financial documentation is important for verifying deductions and maintaining compliance with IRS regulations in the event of a tax audit.

Second Tip: Elect to Be Treated as a Corporation

As we said before, it is an option for owners to elect to be treated as a corporation for tax purposes. It could be beneficial to be treated as an S-Corp in certain situations if owners want to benefit from reducing self-employment taxes, where you can allocate a part of your compensation as a distribution (and not a salary). It can also be beneficial to elect to be treated as a C0-Corp for tax purposes if owners want to benefit from the corporate income tax rate, which is a flat tax that is sometimes lower than the personal tax rate that will be applied to individuals.

Third Tip: Implement Retirement Saving Plans

LLCs can set up their retirement saving plans and can use them to reduce or defer taxes. Different vehicles can be implemented, such as the Solo 401(k)s, the SEP-IRA, the IRA, or the Simple IRA. The contributions made to retirement plans are all deductible from the taxable gross income since they are considered contributions, which have a different tax treatment. It is even more advantageous to make these contributions in years where the taxable gross revenue of the company is high and there is extra cash to invest, otherwise, it would lead to an increase in taxes.

Fourth Tip: Deduct Medical Expenses

In addition to insurance expenses, health insurance premiums are also deductible from the taxable gross income of the company, which can make a big difference while benefiting your members. LLC members can also deduct other medical expenses such as medications, vision expenses, and dental expenses, but also mileage to go to an appointment, to a hospital or even a pharmacy, and more.

Fifth Tip: Contribute to Charitable Causes

Corporations and taxable LLCs can deduct up to 10% of taxable income for charitable contributions. Such contributions can be donations to accredited nonprofit associations, sponsorship of charity events, or inventory given to nonprofit associations. Moreover, if members are not able to deduct all the charitable contributions in the current year (because it was going to represent 10% of the company's taxable gross revenue), they can always carry the contributions over for up to five years. With that strategy, owners are able to deduct 100% of the contributions from the taxable income.

Using tax-saving strategies can be highly beneficial for LLC members. By taking advantage of various eligible deductions, selecting the best tax treatment for their company, choosing the best management structure for their business, and implementing saving plans and charitable contributions, owners can make a tremendous difference in their tax obligations. Ultimately, the choice would depend on the business activity and long-term goals, but many opportunities are available while having an LLC.

Guidance on Reducing Tax Liability Within the Framework of an LLC

Decreasing tax burden within the context of an LLC is possible, but it requires a well implemented tax strategy. Here is some concrete and applicable advice on how LLC members can maximize tax benefits.

- **Understanding Tax Implications:** The first thing for an LLC owner is to understand the different tax treatments available for LLCs and their implications. Because LLCs are pass-through companies, their revenues and losses are not taxed at the corporate level. They appear on the owners' personal tax returns. It avoids double taxation (at the corporate and individual levels). However, as explained before, it is sometimes more beneficial for the LLC to elect to be treated as a corporation, either a S-Corp or a C-Corp. They all have pros and cons, and that is the reason why it is highly advised for LLC owners to consider all options before selecting the one that fits best with their company and long-term goals.

- **Utilizing Deductions:** As explained before, LLC owners should use eligible deductions to lower taxable income. It could be business expenses, such as office rent (even for a home office), supplies, utilities, insurance, and other business expenses. It is highly advised to consult with a tax expert to determine which expenses would be deductible based on the specific business activity and habits, such as home office expenses, travel expenses, and more.

- **Utilizing Tax Credits:** In addition to eligible deductions, LLCs may be eligible for tax credits for certain activities. It could be the R&D tax credit, the Secure 2.0 Act, which offers credits for implementing a 401(k) plan, the natural disaster tax relief, or the Work Opportunity Tax Credit (WOTC), which can be claimed by employers who hire individuals facing barriers to employment. It is advised to consult tax professionals who would tell you precisely what are the tax credits available based on the business activity and specific industry.

- **Implementing Retirement Plans:** As said before, setting up retirement plans, such as the Solo 401(k) or the Simplified Employee Pension (SEP) can result in tax savings for LLC owners. Contributions to these different plans are fully deductible. While providing benefits to themselves, they lower the company's tax burden.

- **Maximizing Depreciation and Amortization:** LLCs can benefit from depreciation and amortization deductions on assets used by the company. LLCs can lower their taxable income and increase their cash flow if they appropriately depreciate assets throughout their useful lives or if they amortize the initial expenses made to acquire them.

Case Studies and Application

Real-life Examples Showcasing Successful Tax Optimization within an LLC

Now that the unique aspects of the tax system of LLCs has been developed, as well as some concrete tips, real-life examples can further explain how some deductions and loopholes can make a tremendous difference in tax savings. Here is some:

Case Study 1: Insurance Premiums Deductions

An LLC can fully deduct health insurance premiums for its employed owners, their spouses, and dependents, which can be very beneficial. Without this deduction, if a family health insurance plan costs for instance $4,000 annually, an owner might have needed to earn as much as $8,000 before taxes. Using an LLC to fully deduct health insurance premiums as a business expense can prevent owners from paying that themselves while reducing the taxable gross revenue.

Moreover, a taxable LLC can buy disability insurance for its employees and deduct the premium. This allows them to benefit from the insurance without having any tax consequences on the premium amount. However, be aware that benefits later received by an employee due to disability would usually be taxable, unless some strategies are implemented to avoid this taxation.

Case Study 2: Business Vehicle Deductions

Like a C-Corp or S-Corp, an LLC can reimburse members for business-related driving expenses, even if they used their vehicle, including the mileage rate. Alternatively, an LLC can also lease a business car, or buy it, and deduct this expense. If the business car is also used for personal use by the LLC member, such as daily commutes, this has to be mentioned in the executive's or employee's Form W-2.

Case Study 3: Home Office Deductions

The IRS regulations allow members and employees of LLC to deduct home office expenses from the taxable gross revenue of the company.

The criteria to qualify as 'home office deductions' are (1) Employees need to consistently and exclusively use their home office for the company's management tasks and administrative tasks; and (2) Employees need to use their home for storing business records, business legal documents, inventory, and product supplies.

LLC members can decide to deduct home office expenses annually or on a monthly basis. It could include expenses such as cleaning services, home utilities, maintenance, phone bills, or even homeowner's insurance. The IRS even approves reimbursement of reimbursement of up to $1,500 for spaces up to 300 square feet without itemizing each expense. However, it is important to remember that when selling your house, the deductions serve as capital gain exclusion up to a certain amount. It is thus advised to avoid home office reimbursement a few years before planning to sell your home.

Case Study 4: Children Employment

As strange as it could be, LLC owners can hire their minor children for after-school work or vacation work and deduct these compensations from the taxable gross revenue. It also offers children a way to set aside money without tax consequences, up to a certain amount fixed by the IRS. They can also use their money to invest in a few retirement plans such as the IRA or Roth IRA.

Case Study 5: Meals and Entertainment Deductions

LLCs can deduct up to 50% of meal expenses for professional events or professional entertainment expenses, as well as 100% of meal expenses for owners and employees. Additionally, employee activities and events, such as Christmas parties, and annual events, are often eligible for 100% deductions.

However, to ensure compliance with tax regulations, it is recommended to keep receipts of your business-related meals, and to write down the purpose of the meal, the persons who attended the meal, and the business relationship. It is also important to note that the IRS is stricter when it comes to alcohol consumption. As a result, consider separating the alcohol expense differently from the meal itself. Furthermore, even if the IRS does not specify a maximum amount per meal, avoid extravagant meals, as the IRS mentions that the meal expense should be "ordinary and necessary."

Case Study 6: Education and Convention Deductions

When employees or owner-employees attend conventions or continuing education events, these expenses are fully deductible from the taxable revenue. It includes travel expenses, accommodation, meals, and even the program fees. Additionally, LLCs can deduct up to $5,250 in education so that owners can enhance or maintain their expertise in a professional field.

For all these expenses, it is important to note that employees do not have to include these benefits in their income, which means that it does not increase their personal taxable income either.

Demonstration of How Specific Tactics Lead to Tangible Benefits for LLCs

In this last section, we will discuss various practical methods that Limited Liability Companies (LLCs) should implement. These tactics are actionable steps that owners should follow to navigate their obligations more easily.

- **State Tax Considerations:** When choosing where to incorporate your LLC, you should consider state tax regulations.

State tax rules differ greatly, and understanding the tax environment in different jurisdictions is critical to making the best choice. For LLCs especially, you have to consider the personal income tax rate in the different states if you decide to continue to be taxed as pass-through taxation or as an S-Corp, and you should consider the C-Corp corporate tax rate in the different states if you consider being elected as a C-Corp. This method can make a tremendous difference from the beginning of the LLC life.

- **Draft a Tailored Operating Agreement:** When it is a multi-member LLC, an operating agreement will outline the rights and responsibilities of each member and will also develop the decision-making processes. It will also provide clarity on the management structure of the company and how the company operates based on its activities. Additionally, it is an opportunity for members to delineate distribution percentages different from the ownership percentages of each member. In the end, drafting a tailored operating agreement is an essential step when establishing an LLC, as it establishes a solid foundation for the business and ensures clarity and transparency among its members.

- **Elect the Best Tax Treatment for the LLC:** As we said before, LLCs are taxed as pass-through entities by default. Even though it can be highly beneficial in some situations, it is sometimes even more beneficial to elect to be treated as a corporation. Consult a professional tax expert who will tell you, based on your industry and long-term goals, what tax treatment would be the most suitable for your LLC. Opting to be taxed as a S-Corp allows members to save in self-employment taxes while electing to be taxed as a C-Corp gives the opportunity to take advantage of the corporate flat tax rate.

- **Deduct As Many Business Expenses:** As detailed above, LLCs can use deductible costs to efficiently lower their taxable gross revenue and lead to significant tax savings. Operating costs, payroll, insurance, travel expenses, supplies, and utilities, are just a few examples of what is feasible. However, it is crucial to maintain compliance with the IRS regulations. That is the reason why owners must keep thorough records of all business-related expenses and should consult tax experts.

- **Amortize and Depreciate Business Assets:** Business assets, such as equipment or real estate investment, can be amortized or depreciated within a certain number of years, which can lead to tax savings for the business. Understanding depreciation schedules and the eligible amortization can help the LLC's cash flow and protect its capital for future projects. It is very recommended to consult a tax expert to implement the right strategies in terms of amortization and depreciation for your business assets.

Unlike other business structures, LLCs provide unique opportunities for tax optimization, personal asset protection and flexibility in the structure and management of the business.

Summary of Key Insights

Investigating tax optimization strategies for small businesses has provided important insight into how owners can maximize their profits while reducing their tax burden. During the course of these three chapters, we have highlighted numerous strategies and concrete methods.

First, to successfully implement tax strategies for their company, business owners must have a solid understanding of the different structures and their tax implications. S-Corporations and Limited Liability Companies have some benefits in common, such as the limited liability company and the pass-through taxation, but they also present differences. S-Corps can help save a lot on self-employment taxes while LLCs provide more flexibility in their tax treatment management, distribution allocation, and less administrative obligations.

Second, both LLCs and S-Corps offer the opportunity to deduct a lot of business expenses. Up to a certain extent, the IRS accepts that owners make deductions of business-related expenses, such as rent, home office equipment and supplies, utilities, and more. Moreover, other specific deductions are feasible depending on the industry and the activity of the business.

The ultimate choice between the two structures will depend on multiple factors. Even though we have tried to go into details as much as possible, the tax regulations are strict in the United States, and it is highly advised to consult a tax expert. These three chapters have made an introduction to the differences between the business structures and their implications on taxation. However, subjective choices, personal preferences, and long-term goals must be taken into account to find the best structure and best tax treatment for your business.

In addition to explaining to you the different options for your business, these chapters have the merit to highlight and enhance the importance of making well-informed decisions as a business owner and how these decisions can have a significant impact on the long-term journey of the business. Additionally, we have to remind you one last time that tax optimization is an ongoing process that requires careful attention and requires owners to stay updated with changes in regulations and tax laws.

CHAPTER 18
CLASSIFICATIONS, REGISTRATIONS, GOVERNMENT CONTRACTS, AND USEFUL TIPS

A	s you can imagine, the cross-section of businesses across the US is vast. For record keeping and data analysis, there has to be a way to accurately classify the type of business. I am not talking about S-Corp or C-Corp or LLC, but the actual industry in which your business operates. The U.S. Office of Management and Budget developed a coding system called the North American Industry Classification System (NAICS), which is used in business industry classification.

It is not necessary to go into the breakdown of every classification, but basically, there are ten categories, within which there are more specific subcategories. The said ten categories are as follows:

- Natural resources and mining

- Construction

- Manufacturing

- Trade, transportation, and utilities

- Information

- Financial activities

- Professional and business services

- Educational and health services

- Leisure and hospitality

- Other services (a type of miscellaneous category if your business does not fall into any of the other categories)

Your business chooses the most appropriate NAICS code for its industry classification, from the extended list. For example, Nursing falls under Educational and Health Services, which uses the code NAICS 623. Within the 623 categories are four sub-sectors identified as

- NAICS 623-1: Nursing Care Facilities

- NAICS 623-2: Residential Retardation, Mental Health, and Substance Abuse Facilities

- NAICS 623-3: Community Care Facilities for the Elderly

- NAICS 623-4: Other Residential Care Facilities

If you have a logistics S-Corp, the category will be Trade, Transportation, and Utilities. If your S-Corp is a catering business, it will fall under Leisure and Hospitality, and so on.

GSA Schedule

GSA is the acronym for General Services Administration, also called the Federal Supply Schedule (FSS), which works via the Multiple Award Schedule (MAS). The modus operandi is for the government to assist corporate companies with government supply contracts on a long-term basis. It is structured as one $45 billion dollar government contract across all industries and regulates pricing and terms of purchase. Basically, the government lays out the rules or qualifying standards, which does make the process more streamlined in a way that you know what to expect. The GSA Schedule is most often interested in contracts with corporations and federal agencies, but state and local governments can also become buyers.

GSA contracts are very valuable, whether your business is an S-Corp or otherwise, which means it is very important to know about how they work. One can look at it as an indefinite supply agreement, and the knowledge that your business is able to have an ongoing supply arrangement does give you peace of mind. The Office of Government Contracting and Business Development lists the following reasons, amongst others, for wanting to buy from smaller corporates:

- to ensure that large businesses do not outmuscle small businesses

- to gain access to the new ideas that small businesses provide

- to support small businesses as engines of economic development and job creation

- to offer opportunities to disadvantaged socio-economic groups

Specific Benefits of a GSA Schedule Contract

As above, the size of the contract means that there is a lot of supply. and service work that the government requires. The sales process is uniform, and it does assist in reducing competition from the point of view that you may have competitors that do not have contracts. Just a note, your business is not restricted to ONLY having government contracts.

What to Consider

If your business has supplied or provided services to the government in the past, getting a GSA contract will be very worthwhile, as be if your competitors have such contracts. Because there is uniformity and regulation to the process, work is fairly distributed. In terms of eligibility, your product or service must fit into one of the GSA Schedule categories, and your financials must reflect how your company is performing financially.

You will have to show evidence that you have a history of providing services effectively if your business is service industry based. Product-based businesses must comply with the Trade Agreement Act, which requires that goods are manufactured in the US or a designated country, falling within the following categories:

- World Trade Organization Government Procurement Agreement Countries
- Free Trade Agreement Countries
- Least Developed Countries
- Caribbean Basin Countries

As you can imagine, the countries that fall within the above four groups are all on standard trading terms with the United States.

Does Your Business Have the Right Resources and Enough of the Right Resources?

You don't want to apply for a GSA contract if your business can't logistically or administratively handle the GSA contract or process. Do an assessment as to whether you have employees and/or employee shareholders that can handle what I will term the back-end or in-office requirements. Then make a call on whether there is enough time to get through the work required to obtain and successfully maintain the contract. You may have to employ someone, and the payoff for that would be getting more income-generating business, which justifies an extra salary.

It has been estimated that it takes between six weeks and six months to obtain a contract, so it may be worth hiring a specialist on a freelance basis to take care of the process. Another reason to use a professional is that it is possible to secure 20-year term contracts, which will be a huge boost for any business whatsoever. Your business may be losing out on work by not having a GSA contract. So if you are in that situation and don't have the resources, you can start putting in place the things that will help you to get a GSA contract.

How to Sell to the Government

If your business has made a decision to get a GSA contract or look into the requirements in more detail, with a view to getting one, there is some background work needed. Committing to the process must be done comprehensively or not at all. My recommendation is to get on it, but here is what to do first.

Research

Firstly, you need to research the market. If your product or service is something that the government does not require or use, then you don't want to waste time going through the process. Fortunately, there is a lot of publicly accessible data on federal contracts. The top four resources to use are USASpending.gov, the Federal Procurement Data System, the Schedule Sales Query Plus, and the GSA eLibrary. You can find all four from a quick Google search. These are the kind of questions you should be looking to answer in this exercise:

- Who is your ideal buyer?

- What does your ideal buyer purchase (what product or service)?

- Who is your ideal buyer purchasing from?

- How does the procurement system work?

The first two are not difficult questions to answer, and prior to starting your business, you should have made comparisons with your competitors, so that information will be at hand. Thus the procurement system knowledge is mainly what you need to arm yourself with.

Registrations

You will have to register as a government contractor, even though you may already have your supply contract in place. If your business was to supply the government in any area, even without a GSA contract, this registration would be necessary. This is what it entails:

DUNS Number

Your business needs to be assigned a code that is then provided to the government in order for procurement-related matters. DUNS is a short form for Dun & Bradstreet Universal Numbering System, and a nine-digit number is an identification number unique to your business.

SAM Registration

The System for Award Management (SAM) is the portal under which several federal systems fall. The one relevant to being a government contractor is the Central Contractor Registration System.

Looking for Government Opportunities

SAM is continuously uploading information on available government work. If you go to SAM.gov, which you will be familiar with after your online registration, you will see several fields that allow you to search via code of industry. Set yourself up to receive email alerts, so you don't miss out on opportunities.

Another contract-finding resource open to GSA Schedule Contract holders is called eBuy. It is an RFQ, or Request for Quote online portal, and your searches will be via your unique codes.

If you have not gone through the registration process or are still busy with it, you could look to subcontract to businesses with existing government contracts. Subcontracting does not provide a direct opportunity, but keep in mind that the business that commissions you to subcontract could very possibly provide your S-Corp with regular work. Such an arrangement is great for learning from a business that is already established in the government sphere, but also for gaining credibility and growing your business. Large contractors with GSA contracts are encouraged to subcontract to smaller businesses as a "helping hand," to put it crudely. Essentially it is to give smaller businesses the ability to be successful, in a large business sphere, or at the least, competitive in that sphere.

DBA (Doing Business As)

This is not a requirement for your S-Corp, but if you are buying into a franchise, then you will probably need to apply for a DBA. Sole proprietorships and partnerships will most often use the term "doing business as," and it is actually legally required in certain states. Back to the franchise scenario, if you buy into a chain of restaurants as an S-Corp, you obviously have to use the name of the franchise. Your S-Corp's legal name may be XYZ Corp, but it would then require a DBA, something like XYZ Corp, doing business as Kentucky Fried Chicken.

In the final part of this chapter, I am going to give you some practical business advice. Parts may seem obvious or just common sense, but these may be things that new business owners take for granted. I have come across people who observe the successes of experienced business owners, who have reached the point in their careers where they don't have to work hard and can enjoy the fruits of their labor. Just remember that these people put in the hard graft for many years to earn an earlier retirement and/or to take a backseat in the running of the business. If it is your goal to get to that point, it probably won't be easy, but remember that the work you put in now will pay off later.

Risks and Rewards

Some people are risk averse, and some get addicted to risk-taking. If you have started your own business, you are prepared to take a risk. When you have made that decision, you will note that other risks will materialize. Earlier I said that you need to be ready and not rush the launch of your business. It may be tempting to try and get your doors open as soon as possible because you want to start securing an income.

If you are employed but intend to resign to set up your own business, do as much as you can while you are still getting an income, and only resign when you get to the point that you have to dedicate more time to the new business than you have available as a full-time employee. This tactic is certainly a mitigation of risk but is not the case in every situation.

The next set of risks will come when your business is operational, and you must consider what the worst possible outcome of a risk could be. Let's say you are a clothing manufacturer, and you have a supplier that offers you a bulk discount if you order X amount of material. You require an increase in the amount of your business loan to make the payment to your supplier. There could be a few different worst cases, but let's say that the worst one is that you pay for the extra supply, get the discount, and make the clothing, but are unable to see half of it as demand is too low. As a result, you struggle to make repayments on the loan, and the discount is outweighed by the lack of turnover and the business loan interest.

In the best-case scenario, you increase the loan, buy the fabric, make the clothing, and sell it. You pay the extra portion of the loan back, and the discount has increased your profit margin significantly. The next step is to look at the practicality. If you have a customer that you can approach and ask if they will be prepared to take a bigger order, and you sign a contract to that effect, your risk has come right down. If that customer is unable to take a bigger order then that risk shoots up again. Yes, you may be able to find another customer that will take some of the extra clothing or even a new customer. However, you know for sure that if you don't buy more stock than usual, you will not have to increase your loan, and you will supply your customer/s as usual.

It all depends on your propensity to take risks. I am not saying do or do not take a risk, but make your decision based on as much information you can gather and the analysis of the possible risk.

Always Look for New Business

We all have some sort of network, and friends, family, and friends of friends or family could all be potential customers. Keep your eyes open and if there is an opportunity in a social setting, for example, then grab it if you can. Think about daily interactions with people and chances to hand out your business card (without being forceful). You may be thinking that business cards are old-fashioned, but they do work (Potters, 2022). Look for free opportunities to promote your business.

There are many groups on social media or otherwise electronically, with the idea of promoting businesses and creating a community that supports each other's businesses. Google Ads are surprisingly cheap, attending conferences is sometimes free, and there is always the giant billboard option. Be as creative as you can!

Maintain Focus and Be Prepared to Put in the Hours

I hate to say it, but things will go wrong. No human in the history of time has gone through their whole life without anything going wrong. Business is the same, and you need to move on from disappointments by staying focused on your business goals.

If you have that drive to succeed, which is evidenced in your focus you will be prepared to work overtime, on holidays, and over weekends. Your staff may not have the same drive, and you may have to pick up the ball where they drop it and fix things. As the adage goes, "you get out what you put in." If you know what you want to get out of your business, you will know what to put in. Always remember that!

Section II Summary

Your S-Corp needs to be allocated an NAICS number, meaning that application must be made to the North American Industry Classification System for an identification number in terms of the classification of the industry that your business falls within. There are ten categories and in each category, there are sub-categories. For example, a catering business would fall under "Leisure and Hospitality."

Government contracts can be obtained via the GSA or General Services Administration, which has the goal of looking after smaller businesses and offering opportunities to socio-economically disadvantaged groups. The government, usually federal but also local, requires a lot of supply of resources, and performance of services, so getting government contracts can aid your business greatly.

The process is quite involved and requires research, so you need to make sure you or your staff can dedicate enough time to it. There are registrations on portals and allocations of specific numbers such as your DUNS number and SAM registration. All the information related thereto is contained in the above chapter. You may need to register a DBA (Doing Business As) if you are an S-Corp that has bought into a franchise.

You need to assess risk and paint the worst-case scenario and the best-case scenario. Assess the variables and what your business stands to gain. Perhaps you will find the risk too great to take, or you may find it an acceptable risk. If your business can handle the worst-case scenario, that is an indication that a potentially serious risk is mitigated, but if your business cannot handle the worst-case scenario, then the risk is not worth taking.

Every business wants more work, so you should be creative with marketing. So many opportunities to market your business in day-to-day life are present. Carry business cards, bring your business up in conversations, use social media, or Google Ads, and as I said earlier, perhaps try the billboard idea.

Maintaining focus is vital, especially when things go wrong, but if you really want your business to succeed, then you will maintain focus, and you will work hard and long to enjoy the rewards in the future.

SECTION III

A DEEP DIVE INTO THE KEY BOOKKEEPING AND ACCOUNTING STRATEGIES FOR LLCS AND S-CORPS

I n the previous section we uncovered how it's very important to make well-informed decisions as a business owner as it is *these* very decisions that can have a lasting impact on the quality of your business long-term.

We guided you step-by-step through the process of setting up your very own LLC or S-Corp, from gathering the required documents to understanding the initial costs and ongoing fees. Whilst also covering the crucial legal and compliance requirements, like drafting operating agreements for LLCs and corporate bylaws for S-Corps, as well as staying on top of state and federal regulations.

With a solid understanding of these foundational elements, you're now ready to delve into the accounting and bookkeeping essentials for your LLC or S-Corp in the next chapter, which is perhaps one of *the* most essential elements of understanding your business. We have already covered some accounting vernacular in chapter 14, however, in this section we are going to dive deeper into the throes of churning numbers, which if done incorrectly, can be highly headache inducing, and we do not want *that* now do we?

As Tilman J. Fertitta wisely advises, *"Don't ever let your business get ahead of the financial side of your business. Accounting, accounting, accounting. Know your numbers"*, this section will explore the critical accounting and bookkeeping strategies tailored for LLCs and S-Corps. By mastering these techniques, you'll be better equipped to maintain financial health, ensure compliance, and drive sustainable growth.

CHAPTER 19
GETTING STARTED WITH
BOOKKEEPING AND ACCOUNTING

W hat does Bookkeeping and Accounting involve? What's the end product? And how are they different? Let's dive in and find out why they're both important for your business in the first place.

Owning an LLC or an S-Corp comes with fantastic legal and financial protections, but to keep these perks, you need to meet certain conditions. Accurate financial records are essential to prove you're compliant with state requirements for LLCs and S-Corps. Without them, you risk losing those valuable protections. Many owners learn this the hard way, but you certainly don't have to! By adopting a consistent approach to your LLC's and S-Corp's accounting and bookkeeping, you'll generate the records needed to defend your entity in court and ensure you enjoy all the benefits of this business structure, further protecting yourself and your business by staying organized and diligent.

Introduction to Bookkeeping

Bookkeeping involves recording and tracking a business's financial transactions. Bookkeepers regularly summarize this activity into reports that reveal the business's performance. They may also handle tasks like invoicing, paying bills, preparing tax returns, monitoring key performance indicators, and offering strategic advice.

To emphasize the importance of bookkeeping it's essential to look at a little historical evidence: Financial record-keeping dates back to ancient civilizations like Mesopotamia, Babylon, Sumer, and Assyria as early as 7000 BC. In ancient Greece and the Roman Empire, archives have revealed accounts tracking farm produce. However, the roots of modern bookkeeping can be traced to the 15th century, with two notable figures credited for documenting the double-entry system. Benedetto Cotrugli is acknowledged for his 1458 book "Of Commerce and the Perfect Merchant," but most consider Luca Pacioli the father of bookkeeping for his 1494 work, "Review of Arithmetic, Geometry, Ratio, and Proportion."

Pacioli, an Italian mathematician and Franciscan monk, provided the first widely-read description of the double-entry system and introduced various bookkeeping tools such as journals and ledgers. His book became the cornerstone of bookkeeping and accounting education for several centuries. By the 1800s, bookkeeping had evolved into a recognized profession in the UK and the US.

Here are some essential bookkeeping concepts and definitions you should know before we move forward. These are fundamental to the methods and processes a bookkeeper uses to create accurate accounts:

Ledger

The ledger serves as the core repository where all financial transactions of a business are methodically recorded and categorized. It acts as a chronological record, documenting every financial event such as sales, purchases, expenses, and payments. For example, a ledger entry might detail a sales transaction where revenue is credited and accounts receivable are debited, reflecting money owed by customers. By maintaining a comprehensive ledger, businesses can track their financial activities with accuracy and clarity.

Accounts

Accounts represent the fundamental classifications under which all business transactions are grouped. These categories include assets (resources owned by the business), liabilities (obligations owed to external parties), equity (ownership interests in the business), revenue (income generated from operations), and expenses (costs incurred to operate the business). Each account serves a specific purpose in the financial ecosystem of the business, facilitating the organization and analysis of financial data. For instance, a business might categorize expenses under various accounts such as rent, salaries, utilities, and supplies to track spending and budget effectively.

Assets

Assets encompass tangible and intangible resources owned or controlled by the business that hold economic value and contribute to future benefits. Examples include cash, inventory, equipment, and accounts receivable (money owed by customers). These assets are vital for sustaining operations and generating revenue. For instance, an increase in inventory reflects the availability of goods for sale, while cash represents liquidity for immediate transactions and financial obligations.

Liabilities

Liabilities denote financial obligations and debts owed by the business to external parties, including suppliers, lenders, and tax authorities. Examples of liabilities include accounts payable (money owed to suppliers for goods or services), loans payable (borrowed funds requiring repayment), and accrued expenses (costs incurred but not yet paid). These liabilities represent essential financial commitments that impact the business's liquidity and financial stability.

Equity

Equity signifies the ownership interests in a business, reflecting the capital contributed by owners or shareholders and retained earnings accumulated over time. It represents the residual interest in assets after deducting liabilities and reflects the business's net worth. For example, an increase in equity may result from capital injections by shareholders or profits retained within the business, enhancing its financial strength and capacity for growth.

Revenue

Revenue constitutes the income earned by the business from its primary activities, such as sales of goods or services, interest on investments, or dividends from investments in other companies. It represents the inflow of economic benefits into the business resulting from its operational endeavors. For instance, a retail business records revenue from sales transactions, indicating the total income generated before deducting expenses and taxes.

Expenses

Expenses encompass the costs incurred by the business in the process of generating revenue and maintaining operational activities. These costs include expenditures on rent, salaries and wages, utilities, raw materials, and administrative expenses. Managing expenses effectively is crucial for controlling costs, optimizing profitability, and ensuring sustainable business operations. For example, a manufacturing company tracks expenses related to production costs, distribution expenses, and administrative overhead to assess operational efficiency and financial performance.

Financial Statements

Financial statements serve as formal records that summarize the financial activities and performance of a business, providing valuable insights into its financial health and operational efficiency. The primary financial statements include the balance sheet, which presents the business's assets, liabilities, and equity at a specific point in time, and the profit and loss (P&L) statement, which outlines the revenue, expenses, gains, and losses incurred over a specific period. These statements enable stakeholders to evaluate the business's profitability, liquidity, and overall financial position.

Balance Sheet

The balance sheet offers a snapshot of the business's financial position by listing its assets, liabilities, and equity as of a particular date. It provides a clear overview of what the business owns (its assets) and what it owes (its liabilities), along with the shareholders' equity representing the owners' stake in the business. For example, a balance sheet might highlight assets such as cash, inventory, and property, liabilities including accounts payable and loans, and equity reflecting capital contributions and retained earnings.

Profit and Loss (P&L) Statement

Also known as the income statement, the P&L statement summarizes the business's revenues, expenses, gains, and losses over a specified period, typically monthly, quarterly, or annually. It calculates the net profit or loss by subtracting total expenses from total revenues, providing crucial insights into the business's financial performance and profitability. For instance, a P&L statement might reveal revenue from sales, cost of goods sold, operating expenses like rent and salaries, and the resulting net income or loss for the reporting period.

Chart of Accounts

The chart of accounts is a comprehensive listing of all accounts used by a business to record its financial transactions in the general ledger. Each account is assigned a unique code or number and categorized under assets, liabilities, equity, revenue, and expenses. It serves as a fundamental tool for organizing financial data and facilitating accurate reporting and analysis. For example, a chart of accounts might include codes for cash accounts, accounts receivable, accounts payable, expense accounts, and revenue accounts, streamlining the process of recording and tracking financial transactions.

Journal Entry

A journal entry refers to the systematic recording of financial transactions in the accounting system, detailing the date, accounts affected, and amounts debited or credited. It serves as the initial step in the accounting cycle, documenting each business transaction accurately and chronologically. For example, a journal entry to record a sales transaction would debit accounts receivable (increasing money owed by customers) and credit sales revenue (increasing income from sales), ensuring the accurate reflection of financial activities in the business's ledger.

These detailed explanations illustrate how each concept plays a crucial role in the accounting and financial management of businesses, providing a foundation for effective decision-making, financial reporting, and regulatory compliance. Understanding these principles is essential for small business owners to maintain accurate financial records, evaluate performance, and achieve long-term financial success.

What is the Difference between Bookkeeping and Accounting?

While bookkeeping primarily focuses on recording financial transactions and maintaining accurate financial records, accounting encompasses a broader set of activities. In accounting, professionals not only *record* transactions but also *analyze, interpret, and communicate* financial information to stakeholders. This includes tasks such as tax planning, financial statement preparation, and auditing, which require a deeper understanding of financial principles and regulations.

In contrast, bookkeepers are primarily tasked with day-to-day recording of transactions and ensuring that financial data is organized and accessible for further analysis by accountants or financial analysts. Thus, accounting involves a more comprehensive range of responsibilities and requires a broader skill set compared to bookkeeping.

We have modern accounting softwares, including cloud-based solutions, that have revolutionized many accounting tasks, enabling many small business owners to manage their accounting independently. Simultaneously, accountants are increasingly relied upon to leverage software effectively, supporting small businesses with their financial management and strategic planning needs.

Small business accounting for your LLC and S-Corps is like the financial GPS for your company, tracking, recording, and analyzing every financial move you make. It's not just about crunching numbers; it's about gaining *insights* into your business's financial health and making informed decisions. Whether you're setting prices, managing inventory, budgeting expenses, planning investments, or plotting growth strategies, accounting provides the data-driven clarity you need. Plus, having a robust accounting process ensures you meet all your legal and regulatory obligations, keeping your business on the right side of the law.

Understanding key accounting terms is crucial for effectively managing your business's financial affairs and communicating with stakeholders. Here's a detailed explanation of each term:

Accounts Payable

Accounts payable represent the outstanding debts a company owes to its suppliers for goods or services received but not yet paid for. For example, if a business purchases inventory on credit terms, the amount owed to the supplier becomes an account payable until it is settled.

Accounts Receivable

Accounts receivable are funds owed to a business by its customers or clients for goods or services provided on credit. This represents revenue that the business has earned but has not yet collected in cash. For instance, a consulting firm invoices a client for services rendered, creating an accounts receivable until the client pays the invoice.

Assets

Assets are tangible or intangible resources owned by a business that hold economic value and are expected to benefit the company in the future. Examples include cash, inventory, equipment, intellectual property, and accounts receivable. These assets contribute to the business's ability to generate revenue and support its operations.

Chart of Accounts

The chart of accounts is a comprehensive listing of all accounts used by a business to record its financial transactions in the general ledger. It categorizes accounts into assets, liabilities, equity, revenue, and expenses, each assigned a unique code or number for systematic recording and reporting purposes.

Equity

Equity represents the ownership interest in a business, representing the difference between its assets and liabilities. It includes contributions made by shareholders (common stock) and retained earnings (profits reinvested in the business). Equity reflects the net worth of the business and is crucial for assessing its financial health and valuation.

Expenses

Expenses are the costs incurred by a business to generate revenue and operate effectively. These costs include salaries, rent, utilities, supplies, marketing expenses, and depreciation of assets. Managing expenses efficiently is essential for controlling costs and maximizing profitability.

General Ledger

The general ledger is the central repository that records all financial transactions of a business. It includes entries for accounts such as assets, liabilities, equity, revenue, and expenses, providing a detailed and organized record of the company's financial activities over time.

Journal Entry

A journal entry is the recording of a financial transaction into the general ledger, consisting of the date, accounts affected, and corresponding debits and credits. It serves as the initial step in the accounting process, ensuring accurate documentation of every financial event, such as sales, purchases, payments, and receipts.

Liabilities

Liabilities represent the financial obligations or debts owed by a business to external parties, including suppliers, lenders, and creditors. Examples include accounts payable, loans payable, accrued expenses, and deferred revenue. Liabilities reflect the company's obligations that must be settled in the future using its assets or earnings.

Revenue

Revenue is the income earned by a business from its primary operations, such as sales of goods or services, interest on investments, and royalties. It represents the inflow of economic benefits into the business resulting from its core activities. Monitoring revenue is crucial for assessing the business's performance and growth potential.

Trial Balance

A trial balance is a report that lists the balances of all accounts in the general ledger at a specific point in time, typically at the end of an accounting period. It ensures that the total debits equal the total credits, verifying the accuracy of recorded transactions before preparing financial statements. A trial balance aids in identifying any errors or discrepancies that need correction before finalizing financial reports.

Understanding these fundamental accounting terms provides small business owners with the knowledge and tools necessary to maintain accurate financial records, make informed decisions, and comply with regulatory requirements. Each term plays a critical role in the financial management and reporting processes, contributing to the overall success and sustainability of the business.

Setting Up Your Accounting System

Setting up your accounting system is a crucial step for managing the financial health of your LLC or S-Corp. It involves choosing the right accounting software, creating a chart of accounts, and establishing financial policies and procedures. Here's a detailed guide on how you can go about establishing a robust system for your LLCs and S-Corps:

Choosing the Right Accounting Software

Accounting software simplifies the process of tracking financial transactions, generating reports, and ensuring compliance with tax regulations. For LLCs and S-Corps, popular options include QuickBooks and Xero.

QuickBooks

QuickBooks is widely used due to its user-friendly interface and comprehensive features tailored for small businesses. It allows you to manage invoices, track expenses, run payroll, and generate financial reports. For example, an LLC operating a retail store can use QuickBooks to track inventory levels, manage supplier invoices, and generate sales reports to analyze performance.

Xero

Xero is another robust accounting software known for its cloud-based functionality, making it accessible from anywhere. It offers features such as bank reconciliation, invoicing, and financial reporting. An S-Corp providing consulting services can use Xero to automate invoice creation, track billable hours, and reconcile bank transactions seamlessly.

When choosing accounting software, consider factors such as ease of use, scalability, integration with other tools, and customer support. Both QuickBooks and Xero offer plans tailored to the needs of small businesses, ensuring you can select a solution that fits your specific requirements.

Creating a Chart of Accounts

A **chart of accounts** (COA) is a structured list of all the financial accounts used by your business. It organizes transactions into categories such as assets, liabilities, equity, revenue, and expenses, providing a clear overview of your financial activities.

Example for an LLC:

- **Assets:**
    - Cash (1010)
    - Accounts Receivable (1020)
    - Inventory (1030)
    - Equipment (1040)
- **Liabilities:**
    - Accounts Payable (2010)
    - Loans Payable (2020)
    - Taxes Payable (2030)
- **Equity:**
    - Owner's Equity (3010)
    - Retained Earnings (3020)

- **Revenue:**

  - Sales Revenue (4010)

  - Service Revenue (4020)

- **Expenses:**

  - Rent Expense (5010)

  - Utilities Expense (5020)

  - Salaries and Wages Expense (5030)

  - Office Supplies Expense (5040)

Example for an S-Corp:

- **Assets:**

  - Cash (1100)

  - Accounts Receivable (1110)

  - Investments (1120)

  - Property, Plant, and Equipment (1130)

- **Liabilities:**

  - Accounts Payable (2100)

  - Accrued Expenses (2110)

  - Deferred Revenue (2120)

- **Equity:**

  - Common Stock (3100)

  - Additional Paid-In Capital (3110)

- Retained Earnings (3120)

- **Revenue:**

  - Product Sales (4100)

  - Consulting Revenue (4110)

- **Expenses:**

  - Marketing Expense (5100)

  - Legal and Professional Fees (5110)

  - Travel Expense (5120)

  - Depreciation Expense (5130)

Developing a detailed chart of accounts customized to fit your business operations is crucial for maintaining precise and organized financial records. This tailored chart not only ensures that all transactions are appropriately categorized but also enhances the clarity and efficiency of financial management and reporting processes.

By structuring accounts to reflect specific revenue streams, expenses, assets, and liabilities relevant to your business, you streamline the tracking of financial activities. This clarity not only simplifies day-to-day accounting tasks but also provides a solid foundation for generating accurate financial statements and insightful business analyses. You do not want to be rifling through a mountain of paperwork just to locate a single statistic. It will truly drive any sane person *entirely* insane (speaking from experience.)

Establishing Financial Policies and Procedures

Establishing clear financial policies and procedures is essential for maintaining consistency, ensuring compliance, and safeguarding your business's financial health. These policies outline how financial transactions are handled, recorded, and reported.

Examples of Financial Policies and Procedures:

1. Expense Reimbursement Policy:

- Define the types of expenses eligible for reimbursement (e.g., travel, office supplies).

- Outline the documentation required for reimbursement (e.g., receipts, expense reports).

- Set a timeframe for submitting reimbursement claims (e.g., within 30 days of incurring the expense).

- Example: An S-Corp may have a policy stating that employees traveling for business must submit travel receipts and a completed expense report within 14 days of returning from the trip.

2. Invoicing and Collections Policy:

- Establish guidelines for creating and sending invoices (e.g., within 2 days of service completion).

- Define payment terms (e.g., Net 30, due within 30 days).

- Outline procedures for following up on overdue invoices (e.g., send reminders after 7 days, follow up with phone calls after 14 days).

- Example: An LLC providing freelance graphic design services might have a policy stating that invoices are to be issued immediately upon project completion, with a 10% late fee applied to payments not received within 45 days.

3. Cash Handling and Banking Policy:

- Define procedures for handling cash transactions (e.g., daily cash counts, secure storage).

- Outline processes for depositing cash into the bank (e.g., daily deposits, dual verification).

- Establish guidelines for reconciling bank statements (e.g., monthly reconciliation by the accounting department).

- Example: A retail LLC may have a policy requiring that all cash received be counted and recorded at the end of each business day, with deposits made to the bank by the following morning.

4. Budgeting and Financial Planning Policy:

- Outline the process for creating annual budgets (e.g., involving department heads, using historical data).

- Define guidelines for monitoring budget performance (e.g., monthly budget reviews, variance analysis).

- Establish procedures for adjusting budgets as needed (e.g., quarterly revisions based on actual performance).

For example, an S-Corp specializing in software development may have a policy requiring quarterly budget reviews to assess project costs and reallocate funds as necessary to stay within budget.

By implementing these policies and procedures, you create a structured framework for managing your business's finances, promoting accountability, transparency, and operational efficiency. Setting up your accounting system correctly from the start lays a strong foundation for your LLC or S-Corp's financial success. Choosing the right accounting software, creating a detailed chart of accounts, and establishing clear financial policies and procedures ensure that your business operates smoothly, remains compliant with regulations, and is well-positioned for growth.

Basic Financial Statements and Their Importance

Financial statements are crucial for understanding the financial health of your LLC or S-Corp. They provide a snapshot of your company's financial position and performance over a specific period. Here's a detailed explanation of the three primary financial statements and how to interpret them, with examples relevant to LLCs and S-Corps.

Balance Sheet

The balance sheet, also known as the statement of financial position, provides a snapshot of your company's assets, liabilities, and equity at a specific point in time. It follows the fundamental accounting equation:

Assets=Liabilities+Equity

Imagine there's an LLC called "Green Thumb Landscaping" on December 30, 2023.

- Assets:

    - Cash: $15,000

- o   Accounts Receivable: $8,000

- o   Equipment: $12,000

- o   Inventory: $5,000

- Liabilities:

- o   Accounts Payable: $6,000

- o   Loan Payable: $10,000

- Equity:

- o   Owner's Equity: $24,000

The balance sheet for Green Thumb Landscaping would look like this:

Balance Sheet (as of December 31, 2023)

Assets	Amount
Cash	$15,000
Accounts Receivable	$8,000
Equipment	$12,000
Inventory	$5,000
Total Assets	$40,000

Liabilities	Amount
Accounts Payable	$6,000
Loan Payable	$10,000
Total Liabilities	$16,000
Equity	**Amount**
Owner's Equity	$24,000
Total Equity	**$24,000**

| Total Liabilities and Equity | $40,000 |

The balance sheet provides a snapshot of your company's financial position. For instance, if Green Thumb Landscaping's total assets are significantly higher than its liabilities, it indicates a strong financial position. Conversely, if liabilities outweigh assets, it may signal potential financial trouble. The equity section shows the owner's or shareholders' stake in the company, reflecting their residual interest after all liabilities are settled.

Income Statement

The income statement, also known as the profit and loss statement (P&L), summarizes your company's revenues and expenses over a specific period, showing the net profit or loss.

Imagine an S-Corp called "Tech Innovators Inc." for the year ending December 31, 2023.

- **Revenue:**
    - Sales Revenue: $150,000
    - Service Revenue: $50,000
- **Expenses:**
    - Salaries: $60,000
    - Rent: $12,000
    - Utilities: $3,000
    - Marketing: $5,000
    - Office Supplies: $2,000

The income statement for Tech Innovators Inc. would look like this:

Revenue	Amount
Sales Revenue	$150,000
Service Revenue	$50,000

Total Revenue	$200,000
Expenses	**Amount**
Salaries	$60,000
Rent	$12,000
Utilities	$3,000
Marketing	$5,000
Office Supplies	$2,000
Total Expenses	**$82,000**

| Net Profit | $118,000|

The income statement reveals your company's profitability over a specific period. For Tech Innovators Inc., a net profit of $118,000 indicates the company is generating more revenue than expenses, signifying a profitable operation. Analyzing revenue and expense trends can help identify areas for cost-cutting or investment to enhance profitability.

Cash Flow Statement

The cash flow statement details the inflows and outflows of cash within your business over a specific period. It is divided into three sections: operating activities, investing activities, and financing activities. Imagine an LLC called "Creative Crafts Co." for the month of January 2024.

- **Operating Activities**:
    - Cash received from customers: $10,000
    - Cash paid to suppliers: $3,000
    - Cash paid for salaries: $2,000
- **Investing Activities**:
    - Purchase of new equipment: $5,000
- **Financing Activities**:
    - Owner's investment: $2,000

The cash flow statement for Creative Crafts Co. would look like this:

Cash Flow Statement (for the month ending January 31, 2024)

Operating Activities	Amount
Cash received from customers	$10,000
Cash paid to suppliers	($3,000)

Cash paid for salaries	($2,000)
Net Cash from Operating Activities	$5,000
Investing Activities	**Amount**
Purchase of new equipment	($5,000)
Net Cash from Investing Activities	($5,000)
Financing Activities	**Amount**
Owner's investment	$2,000
Net Cash from Financing Activities	**$2,000**

| Net Increase in Cash | $2,000 |

The cash flow statement provides insights into the liquidity and cash management of your business. For Creative Crafts Co., a positive net cash from operating activities indicates healthy day-to-day operations. However, a negative cash flow from investing activities due to equipment purchase might be a strategic investment for future growth. Monitoring the net increase or decrease in cash helps ensure the business can meet its short-term obligations.

Understanding and regularly reviewing these financial statements enable LLCs and S-Corps to make informed decisions, plan for growth, and ensure long-term financial stability.

Step-by-Step Guide to Getting Started for LLCs and S-Corps

Starting a business is an exciting journey, but it comes with a multitude of crucial steps to ensure everything is set up correctly from the beginning. You do not want to make grave financial mistakes and set yourself up for failure before you even start. For those choosing to form an LLC (Limited Liability Company) or an S-Corp (S Corporation), the process involves specific actions tailored to these business structures.

Therefore, we have curated an engaging step-by-step guide here that will walk you through registering your business, opening a business bank account, setting up an accounting system, and establishing initial record-keeping practices. By following these steps, you can confidently navigate the early stages of your business, ensuring compliance with legal requirements and setting the stage for financial success. Let's dive into each step with hands-on examples to illustrate how you can effectively get your LLC or S-Corp off the ground.

Step 1: Registering Your Business

The first step in establishing your LLC or S-Corp is to register your business with the state. This involves several sub-steps. Start by choosing your business structure. For instance, Jane decides to form an

LLC for her consulting business due to its flexibility and personal liability protection. She then chooses a unique business name that complies with her state's naming rules, settling on "Bright Future Consulting LLC."

Next, Jane files the Articles of Organization with her state's Secretary of State office for her LLC. This document typically includes the business name, address, the name of the registered agent, and the names of the members. For an S-Corp, the process involves filing Articles of Incorporation, which include similar information but are tailored for corporations. Once her paperwork is filed and approved, Jane obtains an Employer Identification Number (EIN) from the IRS, which is necessary for tax purposes and opening a business bank account.

Step 2: Opening a Business Bank Account

With her business officially registered, Jane proceeds to open a business bank account. This step is vital for separating personal and business finances, which simplifies accounting and offers legal protection. Jane gathers her Articles of Organization, EIN, and her identification documents and heads to her chosen bank. She opens a checking account under "Bright Future Consulting LLC" and deposits her initial capital.

For S-Corps, the process is similar. After registering the corporation and obtaining an EIN, the business owner opens a business bank account, ensuring all financial transactions are conducted separately from personal accounts. This separation is crucial for maintaining the corporation's liability protection and financial integrity.

Step 3: Setting Up an Accounting System

The next step is to set up an accounting system. Jane researches various accounting software options and decides on QuickBooks due to its user-friendly interface and comprehensive features tailored for small businesses. She sets up her chart of accounts, which categorizes all her business transactions. For example, she creates categories like "Revenue," "Expenses," "Accounts Receivable," and "Accounts Payable."

Setting up an accounting system involves not only choosing the right software but also establishing financial policies and procedures. Jane sets policies for expense approvals, invoicing clients, and handling accounts receivable. For S-Corps, accounting software like Xero or QuickBooks can also be effective. The software should be set up to handle payroll, track expenses, and generate financial reports. The owner can set financial policies to ensure consistency and accuracy in financial reporting.

Initial Record-Keeping Practices

Once the accounting system is in place, Jane focuses on initial record-keeping practices. She ensures every financial transaction is recorded accurately and promptly. For instance, when she invoices a client, she enters the details into QuickBooks immediately. When she receives payment, she records it under "Accounts Receivable."

Jane also establishes a routine for reconciling her bank statements with her accounting records monthly. This practice helps her catch any discrepancies early and ensures her financial records are accurate. For S-Corps, maintaining meticulous records is equally important. The business owner should document all financial transactions, including income, expenses, and payroll. Regularly updating and reviewing these records helps in preparing accurate financial statements and tax returns.

To sum it all up, getting started with an LLC or S-Corp involves registering your business, opening a business bank account, setting up an accounting system, and adopting good record-keeping practices. By following these steps diligently, you lay a solid foundation for your business's financial health and compliance with legal requirements.

CHAPTER 20
ESSENTIAL BOOKKEEPING
PRACTICES

Good bookkeeping is the backbone of a well-run business, and for LLCs and S-Corps, it's crucial to establish consistent routines that ensure financial accuracy and compliance. Research has shown that effective bookkeeping practices are directly linked to business success. According to a study by the Small Business Administration (SBA), businesses that maintain accurate financial records are 30% more likely to survive beyond five years compared to those that do not (SBA, 2020). Moreover, a report by SCORE highlights that 82% of businesses fail due to poor cash flow management, which can be mitigated through diligent bookkeeping (SCORE, 2019). This chapter delves into essential bookkeeping practices with detailed, illustrative examples to guide you through daily and weekly tasks.

Daily and Weekly Bookkeeping Tasks

Daily and weekly bookkeeping tasks are essential for maintaining accurate financial records and ensuring the smooth operation of your business. This section outlines key activities that should be performed regularly to keep your books organized and up to date.

Recording Transactions

Recording transactions is a fundamental daily task that involves noting every financial activity your business engages in. For example, Maria owns a small marketing firm structured as an LLC. Every day, she records transactions such as payments received from clients, expenses for office supplies, and any salaries paid out. She uses accounting software like QuickBooks to ensure all transactions are categorized correctly under accounts like revenue, expenses, and accounts payable. This daily practice helps Maria keep her books up-to-date, allowing for accurate tracking of her business's financial health.

Managing Receipts and Invoices

Managing receipts and invoices is another critical task, essential for both daily and weekly bookkeeping. Consider John, who operates an S-Corp called Tech Innovators. Each day, John collects receipts from various purchases and files them into designated folders; either physical or digital. He uses a scanning app to digitize paper receipts, ensuring they're stored securely. Weekly, John reviews all issued invoices to ensure clients have received and processed them. For example, he sends follow-up emails for any outstanding invoices, keeping track of which clients have paid and which haven't. This meticulous management helps

John avoid cash flow issues and maintains a clear record for tax purposes.

Handling Petty Cash

Handling petty cash involves managing small amounts of cash used for minor business expenses, such as office supplies or employee reimbursements. Sarah runs a bakery LLC, and she keeps a petty cash box for day-to-day small expenses. Each time an employee uses petty cash, they fill out a voucher noting the amount and purpose. Sarah reconciles the petty cash weekly by counting the remaining cash and ensuring it matches the total amount of vouchers. For example, if she started the week with $200 and has $120 left with $80 in vouchers, her petty cash is balanced. This practice prevents misuse and ensures accurate financial records.

Therefore, by implementing daily and weekly bookkeeping tasks is vital for the smooth operation of LLCs and S-Corps. Recording transactions daily helps maintain up-to-date financial records. Managing receipts and invoices ensures that you have a clear picture of your income and expenses and that all financial documents are organized. Handling petty cash with strict procedures prevents discrepancies and ensures small expenses are accurately tracked. By consistently following these practices, you establish a strong foundation for your business's financial health and compliance.

Monthly and Quarterly Bookkeeping Tasks

We have already established that effective bookkeeping is crucial for the financial health of any small business. This is why consistent monthly and quarterly bookkeeping tasks ensure that financial records are accurate, up-to-date, and compliant with regulatory standards. These tasks, while sometimes tedious, provide valuable insights into the financial performance of the business and help in making informed decisions. Below, we will discuss key monthly and quarterly bookkeeping tasks including reconciling bank statements, preparing monthly financial reports, and adjusting entries and depreciation.

Reconciling Bank Statements

Reconciling bank statements is the process of comparing your business's financial records with the bank's records to ensure they match. This step is vital to identify any discrepancies, such as unrecorded transactions or errors, which could affect the accuracy of your financial reports. Research has shown that regular bank reconciliation can significantly reduce the likelihood of fraud and errors in financial statements (Smith & Jones, 2022). Here are the steps you can follow to ensure error free reconciliation:

Step 1: Gather Records

Collect Bank Statements: Obtain the bank statements for the period you're reconciling. This could be monthly or quarterly statements, depending on your reconciliation schedule.

Business Transaction Records: Gather your internal financial records, including your general ledger, cash receipts, cash disbursements, and any other documents that record financial transactions.

Step 2: Compare Transactions

Matching Entries: Start by comparing each transaction listed on the bank statement with your business ledger. Look at dates, amounts, and descriptions to ensure they match.

Check Completeness: Ensure that all transactions are recorded in both the bank statement and your ledger. This includes deposits, withdrawals, and any bank fees.

Step 3: Identify Discrepancies

Unrecorded Transactions: Look for transactions that appear on the bank statement but are not recorded in your ledger. These could be bank fees, interest earned, or checks that have cleared.

Outstanding Checks: Identify checks that you have recorded in your ledger but have not yet cleared the bank. These will show up in your ledger but not on the bank statement.

Timing Differences: Recognize that some transactions may be in transit. For example, a payment made towards the end of the month may not be clear until the next month.

Step 4: Adjust Records

Record Missing Transactions: Update your ledger with any transactions from the bank statement that were not previously recorded. This includes bank fees, interest earned, and other miscellaneous transactions.

Correct Errors: If there are any errors in the recorded amounts, correct them. For instance, if a check amount was entered incorrectly in your ledger, update it to match the bank statement.

Record Outstanding Checks: Adjust for checks that have not yet cleared. For example, if you issued a check on the 28th of the month, it might not be clear until the 2nd of the next month. Record these as outstanding checks in your reconciliation.

Step 5: Reconcile Differences

Adjusted Balances: Calculate the adjusted balance for both your ledger and the bank statement. This involves adding any outstanding deposits and subtracting any outstanding checks from your ledger balance.

Match Balances: Ensure that the adjusted balance of your business records matches the adjusted balance of the bank statement. If there are still discrepancies, re-check your entries and calculations.

Final Verification: Once the balances match, you have successfully reconciled your bank statement. Document any adjustments made for future reference and ensure all entries are accurately recorded.

Suppose your bank statement shows a closing balance of $5,000, while your ledger reflects a closing balance of $4,800. To reconcile these balances, start by identifying any outstanding checks. You notice that a check for $300 you issued has not cleared yet, meaning it is recorded in your ledger but not on the bank statement. Next, account for any bank fees; the bank has charged a $20 fee, which appears on the bank statement but has not been recorded in your ledger.

To reconcile the balances, first, adjust the bank balance by subtracting the $300 outstanding check, resulting in an adjusted bank balance of $4,700 ($5,000 - $300). Then, update your ledger to include the $20 bank fee, which adjusts your ledger balance to $4,820 ($4,800 - $20). Finally, compare the adjusted balances: both the bank's adjusted balance and your ledger's adjusted balance now match at $4,700.

This detailed process ensures that all financial records are accurate, identifying and rectifying any errors or discrepancies promptly. Regular reconciliation can prevent financial issues and provide a clear picture of your business's financial health.

Year-End Bookkeeping Tasks

As the year winds down, it's always a good time to dive into crucial year-end bookkeeping tasks that will set your business up for financial success and compliance. This section guides you through the essential steps of closing the books, preparing for tax filing, and conducting a thorough year-end financial review.

Closing the Books

Closing your books involves tidying up your financial records to ensure accuracy and readiness for the new year. Start by reconciling your bank statements with your accounting records. Here's how: compare each transaction on your bank statement with what you've recorded in your books. For example, let's say your bank statement shows a deposit labeled "Client payment," but in your books, it's under "Miscellaneous income." Make sure these match up to avoid discrepancies.

Next, review your accounts receivable and accounts payable. Check outstanding invoices and bills to ensure they're up to date and correctly reflected in your financial statements. If you find any discrepancies, adjust your records accordingly with journal entries. For instance, if a customer's payment was applied to the wrong invoice, correct it promptly to avoid confusion in the future.

Let's consider a more detailed scenario: Let's say you run a small consulting firm. Start by reconciling your bank statements with your accounting records. You notice a client payment of $5,000 labeled as "Consulting Fee" in your bank statement, but it's recorded as "Client Payment" in your books. To reconcile this, update your books to match the bank statement by categorizing it correctly under "Consulting Fee."

Next, review your accounts receivable (AR) and accounts payable (AP). Check your AR aging report and notice an outstanding invoice of $2,000 from a client dated December 28th. Ensure this invoice is recorded in your books for the correct period and adjust accordingly if it's missing. Similarly, review AP to confirm all bills are recorded and paid, especially those due by year-end to properly reflect your financial obligations.

Preparing for Tax Filing

Getting ready for taxes involves gathering all necessary documents and ensuring everything is in order to maximize deductions and minimize headaches. Start by compiling your income statements, balance sheets, and profit and loss statements for the year. Here's a tip: organize your documents by category; like income, expenses, and assets; to make tax preparation smoother.

Double-check your expense categorizations. For example, if you've categorized a business dinner as an entertainment expense, make sure it qualifies as deductible under current tax laws. Keep all receipts and invoices handy to substantiate your claims. If you're unsure about any deductions, consult with a tax advisor to optimize your tax strategy and ensure compliance.

Let's suppose that during your review, you find expenses categorized incorrectly. For example, you categorized a team-building event as "Entertainment Expense" rather than "Employee Benefit." To correct this, update your records to reflect the event's true nature as an employee benefit, which may have different tax implications.

Organize receipts and invoices systematically. For instance, gather all receipts related to office supplies, client meetings, and business travel. Ensure each expense is supported by a receipt or invoice to substantiate deductions claimed on your tax return. This organization not only streamlines tax preparation but also minimizes the risk of missing deductions due to lack of documentation.

Conducting a Year-End Financial Review

A comprehensive financial review helps you understand your business's financial health and plan for the future. Start by calculating key financial ratios like profitability margins and liquidity ratios. Here's how: divide your net income by your total revenue to calculate your net profit margin. Compare this year's margin with previous years to spot trends; like improving profitability or rising costs; that may require attention.

Analyze your cash flow statement to see how money moves in and out of your business. Identify any discrepancies or unexpected expenses that may impact your financial stability. Use this information to develop actionable insights and strategies for the next fiscal year. For instance, if you notice a consistent cash flow issue during certain months, plan ahead with tighter expense controls or explore financing options to bridge the gap.

By following these steps and staying proactive with your year-end bookkeeping tasks, you'll not only ensure financial accuracy and compliance but also gain valuable insights to drive your business forward with confidence in the coming year.

A thorough financial review will always help with assessing your business's financial health and plan for the future. Calculate key financial ratios such as profitability margins and liquidity ratios. For example, compute your net profit margin by dividing net income ($50,000) by total revenue ($200,000), resulting in a 25% margin. Compare this with previous years to track performance trends and identify areas for improvement.

Analyze your cash flow statement to understand how money moves through your business. Suppose your cash flow statement reveals a consistent delay in client payments during certain months, affecting your cash reserves. To address this, implement stricter invoicing and payment policies or explore financing options to improve cash flow management in the upcoming year.

By following these detailed examples and staying proactive with your year-end bookkeeping tasks, you'll ensure financial accuracy, maximize tax advantages, and gain valuable insights to strategically guide your business forward.

Best Practices and Tools for Bookkeeping

Effective bookkeeping is the cornerstone of financial management for any business. This section outlines essential best practices, recommended tools and software, and common pitfalls to avoid maintaining accurate financial records and ensure business success.

Best Practices for Accurate Bookkeeping

Accurate bookkeeping begins with establishing clear and consistent practices. Start by maintaining organized records of all financial transactions, including sales, expenses, and payroll. For instance, always remember to categorize expenses promptly by type; such as office supplies, utilities, and travel; to facilitate easy tracking and reporting. Regularly reconcile bank statements with your accounting records to identify discrepancies early and ensure all transactions are accounted for correctly. Implement robust internal controls to prevent errors or fraud, such as separating duties between recording transactions and approving payments. By adhering to these practices, businesses can maintain financial transparency and make informed decisions based on reliable data.

Recommended Tools and Software

Utilizing reliable tools and software streamlines bookkeeping tasks and enhances efficiency. Consider using accounting software like QuickBooks or Xero, which automate processes such as invoicing, expense tracking, and financial reporting. These platforms offer features like bank reconciliation and integration with business bank accounts, reducing manual errors and saving time.

For example, QuickBooks allows you to generate customizable financial reports that provide insights into cash flow, profitability, and tax liabilities. Additionally, cloud-based solutions ensure accessibility from anywhere, facilitating collaboration with accountants or team members remotely. Select tools that align with your business needs and scalability to support growth while maintaining accuracy and compliance.

Common Pitfalls and How to Avoid Them

Avoiding common pitfalls in bookkeeping is essential for maintaining financial accuracy and compliance. One significant pitfall is the **mixing of personal and business finances.** When personal and business expenses are commingled, it becomes challenging to accurately track business expenses for tax purposes. For instance, imagine a small business owner using their personal credit card for business purchases such as office supplies and client lunches.

Without clear separation, distinguishing deductible business expenses from personal expenditures becomes cumbersome during tax preparation. To mitigate this issue, it's crucial to establish separate bank accounts and credit cards specifically for business transactions. This separation not only simplifies reconciliation but also ensures that all business expenses are properly documented and accounted for, reducing the risk of tax filing errors and potential audits.

Another common pitfall is **neglecting regular backups of financial data.** Businesses that fail to implement reliable backup systems risk losing critical financial information in the event of system failures, data breaches, or natural disasters.

Consider a scenario where a business's computer system crashes, resulting in the loss of essential financial records and transaction histories. Without backups, recreating this information can be time-consuming and may lead to inaccuracies in financial reporting and compliance. To safeguard against such risks, businesses should invest in automated backup solutions or utilize secure cloud storage services. These technologies ensure that financial data is regularly backed up and accessible from multiple locations, minimizing downtime and preserving data integrity in adverse situations.

Furthermore, **staying informed about tax regulations and compliance requirements** is crucial to avoid penalties and ensure financial health. Tax laws are dynamic and subject to frequent updates, making it essential for businesses to stay abreast of changes that may affect reporting obligations or tax liabilities. For example, failing to claim eligible deductions or missing filing deadlines can result in unnecessary financial burdens and regulatory scrutiny. To mitigate these risks, businesses should maintain regular communication with tax advisors or accountants who can provide guidance on compliance issues, tax planning strategies, and upcoming regulatory changes.

By proactively educating themselves on tax laws and implementing sound financial practices, businesses can minimize risks, optimize tax efficiency, and foster long-term growth and success.

By adopting best practices such as separating personal and business finances, implementing robust backup systems, and staying informed about tax regulations, businesses can enhance their bookkeeping efficiency, maintain accurate financial records, and make informed decisions that support sustainable growth and success.

These proactive measures not only mitigate potential pitfalls but also strengthen financial management practices, ensuring resilience and compliance in a competitive business environment.

Additional Measures You Can Take to Protect Yourself Against Losses

Safeguarding against losses is a critical aspect of financial management that involves implementing robust controls and practices to protect assets and mitigate risks. Accountants play a pivotal role in ensuring these safeguards are effectively implemented within an organization. Here's an elaboration on the types of controls and practices typically used:

Segregation of Duties

Segregation of duties is a fundamental control mechanism aimed at preventing fraud and errors by dividing responsibilities among different individuals. For example, in a small business, the person responsible for purchasing inventory should not also be tasked with paying invoices. By separating these functions, businesses reduce the risk of unauthorized payments or misappropriation of funds. This segregation ensures that multiple individuals are involved in critical financial processes, providing checks and balances that enhance accountability and transparency.

Assignment of Authority

Delegating authority involves defining roles and setting limits on purchasing and spending activities within an organization. For instance, businesses may establish spending thresholds and require authorization from designated personnel for purchases exceeding certain amounts. By clearly delineating authority levels and approval processes, organizations maintain control over expenditures and prevent unauthorized or excessive spending. This practice ensures that financial decisions align with organizational goals and budgetary constraints, promoting fiscal discipline and resource efficiency.

Safety of Assets

Protecting financial and other assets is essential to safeguard against theft, loss, or unauthorized access. This includes physical security measures such as restricting access to cash, locking doors, and securing sensitive financial documents and equipment. For example, businesses may implement security protocols for handling cash transactions, such as using safes or cash registers with limited access. Additionally, promptly depositing checks into designated bank accounts minimizes the risk of loss or misplacement. By prioritizing asset security, organizations mitigate operational risks and uphold financial integrity.

Performance Measurement

Performance measurement involves establishing benchmarks and accountability mechanisms to evaluate operational effectiveness and financial outcomes. This includes monitoring key performance indicators (KPIs), conducting regular audits, and performing reconciliations to verify the accuracy and reliability of financial reports. For instance, businesses may track inventory turnover rates to assess inventory management efficiency or conduct financial audits to ensure compliance with regulatory standards and internal policies. By holding individuals accountable for their responsibilities and performance results, organizations foster a culture of accountability and continuous improvement.

Verifications

Verifications are critical steps that ensure reported numbers and financial data are accurate and reliable. This includes conducting audits, inventory checks, and reconciliations to validate transactions and account balances. For example, periodic inventory audits help businesses identify discrepancies between physical inventory counts and recorded inventory levels, preventing inventory shrinkage or discrepancies due to theft or errors. Similarly, reconciling bank statements with accounting records ensures that all transactions are properly recorded and discrepancies are promptly addressed. By performing thorough verifications, organizations enhance financial transparency, mitigate risks of errors or fraud, and maintain trustworthiness in financial reporting.

Thus, by implementing controls such as segregation of duties, delegation of authority, security measures, performance measurement, and verifications, accountants can effectively safeguard against losses, protect assets, and uphold financial integrity within organizations. These practices not only mitigate risks associated with fraud and errors but also promote efficiency, accountability, and sustainable growth in today's dynamic business environment.

Section III Summary

This section introduced the essential concepts of accounting and bookkeeping, highlighting their importance in managing a business's finances. Accounting involves recording, classifying, summarizing, and interpreting financial transactions, providing insights into a business's financial health. Bookkeeping focuses on the systematic recording of daily transactions. We also highlighted the importance of setting us an effective accounting system for small business owners.

This is because choosing the right accounting software, such as QuickBooks or Xero, is crucial as these platforms offer user-friendly interfaces and comprehensive features tailored for small businesses. Creating a detailed chart of accounts helps in organizing financial information systematically. Additionally, establishing financial policies and procedures ensures consistency and accuracy in financial reporting, laying a solid foundation for effective financial management.

Understanding basic financial statements is critical for any business owner. The three primary financial statements: the balance sheet, income statement, and cash flow statement. The balance sheet provides a snapshot of the company's financial position at a specific point in time, detailing assets, liabilities, and equity. The income statement shows the company's performance over a period, highlighting revenue, expenses, and net profit or loss. The cash flow statement tracks the flow of cash in and out of the business, which is essential for managing liquidity.

This section conveys practical insights that aim to new business owners through the initial steps of establishing their business's financial management system. It starts with registering the business and obtaining the necessary licenses. Opening a dedicated business bank account is emphasized to separate personal and business finances. Setting up an accounting system involves choosing appropriate software, creating a chart of accounts, and establishing initial record-keeping practices. These steps are crucial for maintaining accurate financial records and ensuring compliance with regulatory requirements.

Furthermore, daily and weekly bookkeeping tasks are vital for maintaining up-to-date and accurate financial records. This second chapter emphasizes recording all financial transactions promptly, managing receipts and invoices, and handling petty cash. Monthly and quarterly tasks involve more detailed activities such as reconciling bank statements, preparing monthly financial reports, and making adjusting entries to account for depreciation. Year-end bookkeeping tasks are critical for closing the books and preparing for tax filing. This includes ensuring all transactions are recorded and reconciled, organizing financial records, and conducting a year-end financial review to evaluate business performance.

We also gave you valuable insights pertaining to the best practices in bookkeeping, recommending tools and software to streamline tasks and discussing common pitfalls to avoid. Thus, providing you with a comprehensive action plan for implementing a bookkeeping system, including daily, weekly, monthly, and year-end checklists. Developing consistent record-keeping habits is emphasized as crucial for maintaining accurate and up-to-date financial records, essential for the business's success and regulatory compliance.

GLOSSARY

Articles of Incorporation: Legal documents with your business details are to be filed with your state IRS office.

C-Corp: C-Corporation—Legally recognized types of corporation.

CCRS: Central Contractor Registration System—Where your business is registered as a government contractor.

DBA: Doing Business As—If the name of your business is different from the registered name, it is classified as DBA.

DUNS: Worldwide identification number for your business.

EIN: Employer Identification Number—Mandatory number identifying your business as an employer; received on application to the IRS.

Expenses: Total amount of money paid out for the year.

FSS: Federal Supply Schedule—GSA is also referred to as the FSS.

GSA: General Services Administration—Online system that controls government supply contracts given to businesses.

IRS: Internal Revenue Service—The government body responsible for taxation.

LLC: Limited Liability Company—Legally treated as a corporation or partnership.

LLP: Limited Liability Partnership—A partnership that is registered for limited liability. Usually a group of professionals, such as lawyers or doctors.

MAS: Multiple Award System—Interface on the GSA system.

NAICS Code: North American Industry Classification System Code—A unique code that identifies what economic sector a business falls into.

Payroll taxes: Tax on salaries.

Profit: Money received less money paid out (including salaries).

QBI: Qualified Business Income Deduction—Certain income is subject to tax deductions as per the IRS.

Revenue: Total amount of money received for the year.

RFQ: Request for Quotation.

SAM: System for Award Management—Portal for the awarding of government contracts.

S-Corp: S-Corporation—Legally recognized types of corporations.

Sole Proprietorship: An owner-run business.

ADDENDUM: CHECKLIST

The below checklist should be useful in consolidating the steps you need to take in order to get your S-Corp up and running. It doesn't only contain the admin parts, but some useful information in an ordered layout:

- Ascertain whether your business meets the qualifying requirements as discussed in chapter one.

- Consider whether you will benefit from the pass-through tax, taking into account the salaries that you intend to pay. Use the tables in chapter two, to provide assistance.

- Follow the seven-step process covered in chapter three, i.e.

  - Decide on a name

  - Check if the name is available

  - Choose your preferred state

  - File articles of association

  - Appoint a board of directors

- Keep minutes of all meetings

- Apply for your businesses Employee Identification Number

- If you are converting an LLC, decide on statutory conversion, the merger of non-statutory conversion (not recommended due to complication and cost).

- Consider using a company that specializes in creating S-Corps. See the list of recommended companies in chapter three.

- Look at different financing options.

- Draw up an operating agreement, so that all parties involved know where they stand and what is expected of them.

- Things to avoid:

  - no business plan

  - disorganization

  - not defining your target market

  - not signing contracts

  - wasting money

  - incorrectly valuing your product or service

- Decide on your method of accounting (cash or accrual), and make sure you update your books regularly.

- Make sure you understand your tax requirements as set out in chapter five. Appointing a professional to assist in this department is highly recommended.

- Use chapter six to familiarize yourself with government contracts, the necessary registrations, and the requirements for becoming a government contractor.

- Work hard, put in the hours, and reap the rewards.

CONCLUSION

I hope that you have enjoyed this book and have taken out of it what you expected to. You should, by this point, have established whether an LLC or an S-Corporation will suit your particular business. If you are of the opinion that LLC or S-Corporation is not the right vehicle for your business, then you should have an understanding of the other options open to you. The best way to conclude this book is to extract the main points, sequentially, so that you can be reminded of the nuts and bolts, and also so that you can refer back to the sections of interest.

An LLC, or Limited Liability Company, stands as a beacon of flexibility and protection for entrepreneurs navigating the tumultuous seas of the business world. This business structure elegantly combines the pass-through taxation of a partnership or sole proprietorship with the limited liability of a corporation, offering a shield to its owners (known as members) against personal liability for the company's debts and obligations. Its inherent versatility allows for an unlimited number of members, and it can be managed by these members or appointed managers, catering to various operational styles and business needs. The

LLC model has emerged as an exceedingly popular choice for those seeking to embark on their entrepreneurial journey with confidence, knowing their personal assets are safeguarded while they explore the vast potential of their business ventures.

Forming an LLC is a strategic step that involves several key stages. Initially, you must select a unique name that complies with state-specific guidelines and is distinct from existing entities. Here are the steps mentioned briefly. For more details please refer to chapter three:

1. Choose a unique name for your LLC that adheres to your state's naming requirements and distinguishes your entity from others.

2. File the "Articles of Organization" with the relevant state office and pay the applicable state fee.

3. Draft an operating agreement to establish the LLC's operational guidelines, profit-sharing, and management structure.

4. Obtain any business licenses or permits required to legally operate your LLC.

5. Comply with tax regulations by securing an Employer Identification Number (EIN) from the Internal Revenue Service (IRS).

Moreover, an S-Corp is made up of shareholders and is limited to 100 individuals and one class of stock. Ownership is directly in line with percentage shareholding, and shareholders are taxed in their personal capacity. This is referred to as a pass-through tax, which means that there is no double taxation on the S-Corp and the shareholders. A major advantage is the limitation of liability, in that shareholders enjoy the protection of their personal assets.

There are seven steps to be followed when forming an S-Corp, I will list them below, but for the full breakdown, you will have to look at chapter twelve:

- Decide on a name

- Check that the name is available

- Choose your state

- File and submit your articles of association (example template provided)

- Establish your board of directors

- Keep minutes of meetings

- Get your Employee Identification Number and make your tax status election

In terms of set-up, you can do a statutory conversion, also called a quick-status conversion, during which you file with the secretary of state. If you want to give your LLC S-Corp status, you will use a statutory merger, upon which the members will vote before filing. The least popular option is a non-statutory conversion, during which you will have to hire lawyers and accountants to create a corporation, transfer assets and liabilities, then liquidate and dissolve your LLC.

There are companies that will attend to the set-up for a fee, and they are listed under the particular section in chapter three.

Financing your business can be done via several methods. My recommended method is using a business lending marketplace, which is a one-stop shop when it comes to finding financing options. You only have to fill out one application form, which will then give you access to information on loans from a variety of lenders. I recommend

Lendio.com. You will then be able to go through the options and decide which will work best for your business.

An operating agreement is not a stringent requirement, but it is wise to have one signed by all parties, and record the terms of the business relationship between the shareholders. Mistakes in life are inevitable, and the same applies to business, but if you are aware of possible mistakes, you can avoid them or at least mitigate the backlash if they do happen. You can't be afraid of failure, you have made your decision, and you have to back yourself. Don't neglect to make a business plan, part of which will define your target market. It is also not advisable to do everything yourself. It is worth paying experts in order to save time and prevent future problems. You don't want to get the wrong investors or the wrong employees.

So, do your due diligence in those regards. Understand what you need in terms of capital investment. My advice is to include a 20% contingency for unforeseen costs. Avoid wasting money, and not valuing your product correctly. You don't want to sell yourself short, but you also shouldn't be greedy. Don't get ahead of yourself by launching too early, trying to expand too quickly, and hiring too quickly. Lastly, do not make the mistake of neglecting to create a marketing plan. Here is a reminder of the components of a good plan:

- business mission

- key performance indicators

- your target market

- identify your competition

- your specific strategies and budget

Bookkeeping and keeping and accounting are two aspects that you need to stay on top of. It is best to update your books regularly and keep copies of absolutely anything that forms proof of transactions.

Section 3 covers the fundamental concepts of accounting and bookkeeping, emphasizing their importance in managing a business's finances. Accounting involves recording, classifying, summarizing, and interpreting financial transactions to provide insights into a business's financial health. Bookkeeping, on the other hand, focuses on recording daily financial transactions. This section also covers the differences between accounting and bookkeeping, practical guides and highlights how each function supports business operations.

Lastly, three pieces of advice to remember in starting up and running a successful business. Analysis of risk and reward could make or break your business. Bad decisions have sent many businesses under. The simplest way of looking at it is in question form: Can my business cope if the risk does not pay off and the absolute worst result happens? If the answer is yes, then the risk may be justified. If the answer is no, then that risk is not worth taking (Potters, 2022).

Always be on the lookout for new business, whether it be in social situations, at conferences, on social media, or any other form of advertising platform. You have got to maintain focus and be prepared to work hard. When things go wrong, and you need to fix them, you must call upon your focus when you have to work weekends and holidays. If you go in half-heartedly, then your success will be limited. So on top of choosing the right business entity, you have to make the choice to put in everything you have.

I would like to leave you with a quote that you can remember if things get tough or you encounter seemingly insurmountable problems. The quote is from Nelson Mandela, freedom fighter and Nobel peace prize winner:

"It always seems impossible until it's done."

REFERENCES

§1.1244(c)-1 26 CFR Ch. I (4-1-20 Edition) - Govinfo.gov. www.govinfo.gov/content/pkg/CFR-2020-title26-vol13/pdf/CFR-2020-title26-vol13-sec1-1244c-1.pdf.

Akalp, N. (2021, August 10). LLC. Which LLC Is Right for Me? (corpnet.com)

Berry-Johnson, J. (2022, January 3). Corporation: What is it and How to Form One? https://www.investopedia.com/terms/c/corporation.asp

Articles of incorporation. (2022, March 17). Legaltemplates. https://legaltemplates.net/form/articles-of-incorporation/

Bajpai, P. (2022, July 16). *Understanding S Corporations.* Investopedia. https://www.investopedia.com/articles/investing/091614/understanding-s-corporations.asp

Bryniarski, B (2020). *S Corporation Reasonable Compensation.* AICPA. https://www.aicpa.org/resources/article/s-corporation-reasonable-compensation

Chi, C. (2022, December 8). *What is a Marketing Plan and How to Write One.* Blog.hubspot. https://blog.hubspot.com/marketing/marketing-plan-examples

Crail, C. Haskins, J. Watts, R. (2022, July 8). What is a Limited Liability Company (LLC)? Definition, Pro's and Con's. What Is An LLC? Definition, Pros & Cons – Forbes Advisor

CT Corporation Staff. (2022, June 3). What are S-Corporations: Key Benefits and More. Wolterskluwer. https://www.wolterskluwer.com/en/expert-insights/s-corporations#:~:text=Because%20of%20pass%2Dthrough%20taxation,(e.g.%2C%20the%20shareholders)

Glenn, D. (2022, May 9). *4 Things Doctors Should Consider Before Using an S-Corporation.* Taxcpafordoctors. https://www.taxcpafordoctors.com/4-things-doctors-should-consider-before-using-an-s-corporation/

GMP – Government Marketing & Procurement, L. (2021, July 15). *GSA schedules explained* - GMP - government marketing & procurement, LLC. https://www.gmpgov.com/gsa-schedules-explained/

Gonzalez, E. (2022, May 18). *Pros and Cons of S-Corps vs. C-Corps.* Fool. https://www.fool.com/the-ascent/small-business/document-management/articles/s-corp-vs-c-corp/

GSA. (2020, April 15). *TAA Designated Countries.* https://gsa.federalschedules.com/resources/taa-designated-countries/

Haskins, J. (2022, August 2). *Can I Change my LLC to an S-Corporation.* https://www.legalzoom.com/articles/can-i-change-my-llc-to-an-s-corporation#:~:text=to%20S%20corp.-,How%20to%20Change%20from%20LLC%20to%20S%20Corp.,an%20officer%20of%20the%20company.

Haskins, J. (2022, May 2). LLC vs Corporation: Which One is Right for Me? LLC vs. Corporation: Which One is Right for Me? | LegalZoom

Haskin, J. (2022, May 2). 6 Steps to Filing Corporation Taxes. https://www.legalzoom.com/articles/6-steps-to-filing-corporation-taxes.

History.com, editors, various. (2010, April 9). John D. Rockefeller. https://www.history.com/topics/early-20th-century-us/john-d-rockefeller

History.com, editors, various. (2009, November 9). Andrew Carnegie. https://www.history.com/topics/19th-century/andrew-carnegie

Hurston, H. (2020, July 20). *S Corp Advantages and Disadvantages*. Wolterskluwer. https://www.wolterskluwer.com/en/expert-insights/s-corporation-advantages-and-disadvantages

Indeed Editorial Team. (2020, April 17). *6 Primary Types of Corporations and Their Differences*. Indeed. https://www.indeed.com/career-advice/career-development/types-of-corporations

Jefferson, R. (2020, August 25). 4 Common Mistakes That People Make When Running an LLC. 4 Common Mistakes People Make When Running An LLC – Lawyers Rock

Journals, B. (n.d.). *Should your startup become an S-Corp*. Brex. https://www.brex.com/journal/s-corp

Kappel, M. (2022, November 9). *How to Form a C-Corp*. Patriotsoftware. https://www.patriotsoftware.com/blog/accounting/form-c-corp/

Kopp, C. (2022, December 18). *Partnership: Definition, How It Works, Taxation, and Types*. Investopedia. https://www.investopedia.com/terms/p/partnership.asp#:~:text=A%20partn ership%20is%20an%20arrangement,form%20a%20limited%20liability%20p artnership.

Kopp, CM. (2022, June 15). *Partnership: Definition, How it Works, Taxation, and Types*. Investopedia. https://www.investopedia.com/terms/p/partnership.asp

Majaski, C. (2022, October 15). *LLC vs. S Corporation:* What's the Difference? Investopedia. https://www.investopedia.com/articles/personal-finance/011216/s-corp-vs-llc-which-should-i-choose.asp

Martins, A. (2022, August 12). Which LLC Taxes Must Your Business File. LLC Tax Guide - businessnewsdaily.com

Miller, MK. (2021, April 26). *5 Things You Should Know About Using a Lending Marketplace*. Lendio. https://www.lendio.com/blog/5-things-know-about-using-lending-marketplace/

Murphy, K. (2022, August 15). Small Business Accounting: How to Set Up and Manage Your Books. Small Business Accounting 101: Basics, Set Up, Software (2022) (shopify.co.uk)

Murray, J. (2022, September 11). How do I Calculate Estimated Taxes for my Business? How Do I Calculate Estimated Taxes for My Business? (thebalancemoney.com)

Organ, C. Main, K. (2022, August 18). How to Change a Sole Proprietorship to an LLC in 6 Steps. https://www.forbes.com/advisor/business/how-change-sole-proprietorship-to-llc/

Pash, A. (2022, February 26). *NAICS Codes: What Do They Mean For Your Business.* https://pricereporter.com/naics-codes-what-do-they-mean-for-your-business/?gclid=CjwKCAiA-dCcBhBQEiwAeWidtahUX_f8KduMRi_BivxmsYrjxd5YXjI5ExvWDgRUL wGNnkopjGaZYBoCBwkQAvD_BwE

Pierce, M. (n.d.). *S Corp - Single Class of Stock Rule.* https://wyomingllcattorney.com/Incorporate-a-Wyoming-Corporation/S-Corp-Single-Stock-of-Class-Rule

Potters, C. (2022, July 3). *How to Grow a Successful Business.* Investopedia. https://www.investopedia.com/articles/pf/08/make-money-in-business.asp

Prakash, P. (2022, March 31). *DBA (Doing Business AS): What is it and How do I Register?* Nerdwallet. https://www.nerdwallet.com/article/small-business/dba-doing-business-as

Research Team, Knowledge Hub. (2022, April 26). Everything You Need to Know About Accounting for an LLC. Everything You Need to Know About Accounting for an LLC (generisonline.com)

Rosenberg, E. (n.d.). *How to Run Payroll for an S-Corp.* Collective. https://www.collective.com/blog/money-management/scorp-payroll/

Small Business Administration. (n.d.). Retrieved Feb 10, 2024, from https://www.sba.gov/

S corp operating agreement: UPCOUNSEL 2023. (n.d.). https://www.upcounsel.com/s-corp-operating-agreement#:~:text=July%202%2C%202020%3A-,An%20S%20corp%20operating%20agreement%20is%20a%20business%20entity%20managing,of%20organizing%20the%20business%20operation.

SCORE. (n.d.). Retrieved Feb 10, 2024, from https://www.score.org/

Schooley, S. (2022, August 10). *20 Mistakes to Avoid When Starting a Business.* Businessnewsdaily. https://www.businessnewsdaily.com/7398-startup-mistakes-to-avoid.html

Sember, B. (2022, July 28). Which State Should You File Your LLC in? Which State Should You File Your LLC In? | LegalZoom

Silver, C. Attkinson, A. Woosley, B. Kagan, J. Chaturvedi, V. Wrenn, S. Alpert, C. Halton, C. Feldman, J. Laidley, C. Williams, W. (2021, July 30). What is the History of Corporations in America? https://www.investopedia.com/ask/answers/041515/what-history-corporations-america.asp#:~:text=The%20first%20American%20corporations%20were,development%20like%20the%20United%20States.

Treece, K. (2022, December 2). *Best Startup Business Loans of December 2022.* Forbes. https://www.forbes.com/advisor/business-loans/best-startup-business-loans/

Unknown. (2022, June 2). *Everything About S Corporation Formation in 2022.* https://www.offshorecompanycorp.com/insight/jurisdiction-update/everything-about-s-corp-formation-in-2022?gclid=Cj0KCQiAkMGcBhCSARIsAIW6d0CbjgvLkXZwtgtjd-FDe2xQVtN0VFuzZ5Ba2-JdCPt4_MyOBWV_OMgaAmRvEALw_wcB

Upcounsel. (2020, June 28). *Issuing Shares in an S-Corporation: What You Need to Know.* https://www.upcounsel.com/issuing-shares-in-an-s-corporation

UpCounsel Technologies, various authors (2022, month and date unknown). Explain LLC: Everything You Need to Know. Explain LLC: Everything You Need to Know (upcounsel.com)

Unknown Author. (2019, March 28). Small Business Accounting 101: A Ten Step Guide for Financial Success. Small Business Accounting 101 | a 10-Step Guide for Financial Success (freshbooks.com)

Watkins, P. (2022, July 5). *Why Should You Convert Your LLC to an S-Corporation?* Novo. https://www.novo.co/blog/switch-from-llc-to-s-corporation

Watts, R. Haskin, J (2022, July 8). How to Effectively Dissolve an LLC. How To Dissolve An LLC – Forbes Advisor

Watts, R. Haskins, J. (2022, September 4). How to Set Up an LLC in 7 Steps. How To Set Up An LLC In 7 Steps – Forbes Advisor

Wong, B. (2022, May 2). Should You Convert Your Corporation to an LLC? Should You Convert Your Corporation to an LLC? | LegalZoom

Woodman, C. (n.d.). *How to Keep Accounting Records for an S-Corporation.* Smallbusiness.chron. https://smallbusiness.chron.com/close-expense-account-57887.html

Made in United States
Orlando, FL
29 December 2024